Social Media Content

The best process and mindset for dealing with Content

SOCIAL MEDIA CONTENT

The Goal

I always say there are 4 key elements to be taken into consideration with any good marketing campaign.

- Purpose,
- Effectiveness,
- On Brand,
- Return on Investment.

We are in an age where to stay relevant in the digital marketing space everything is Content, Content, Content. It puts a lot of burdens on your marketing team and more so on yourself if your a small business owner.

With this book I am hoping to help outline the best process and mindset for approaching, creating, publishing and analysing your content. To help eliminate the stress and make it a more manageable and enjoyable task and one in which you can start seeing some positive results both in terms of social engagement and increased volumes and rate of conversions

First Published 2019
All Content Copy Right 2019 Ryan Wakeman

RYAN WAKEMAN

The Author

I got into Web Design and IT from an early age, became marketing manager for a national company and then fell in love with nightclubs and business.

I then learnt:

Build from your core skill set
I was fortunate with the turns of events which structured my core skill set and this became a great foundation to adapt and digress to apply to other projects.

Never Grow Up
Toy's ain't just for children, stay active and learn to do what's fun. Maybe why I deem it acceptable to race around on a 20 mph electric skateboard.

Believe Pigs can Fly
The impossible just makes life more fun, think of a challenge and make it that bit harder. Once when driving across Europe back to Calais, traffic was against me and it was becoming a slog of a drive. So I logged on and made my crossing an hour earlier to help keep the focus and make it a bit more entertaining.

Over the years I've worked within various different industries however slightly weighted towards Leisure and Hospitality, often consulting from a business and marketing perspective.

Me and a friend took the plunge and opened a restaurant chain. In the process we found establishing a strong and engaging social media audience for our business made the world of difference while developing, pushing new products and for driving footfall.

Currently I spend a lot of time working with others to help refine their approach to content creation and seeing the same things time and time again is what prompted me to write this book. I won't lie writing a book is something I've wanted to do for a while and with this being a topic I live and breath it seemed to make sense.

Contents

Intro

Mindset for Creating Content — 10

Section One - Approach

Don't be a bull in a china shop — 24

Where are we posting? — 28

Where are sending our customers? — 37

What can we achieve? — 42

Types of Content we can create — 48

Benefits of Blogging — 58

Section Two - Plan

What are we promoting? — 64

How often are we posting? — 67

Choosing our Themes	75
Making a List of Messages	80
Consideration of Paid Campaigns and Specific Targeting	94
Marrying our prospective Content with our Schedule	99

Section Three - Create

Creating Content for our Schedule	106
Tools / Do we Outsource	108
Plan Sessions for Creating Content	114
But could you Cheat	121
Edits / Post Production	124

Section Four - Publish

Do we use Automated Tools (Pros & Cons)	132
Interim Content and Changes	138
Links and Short Links	142

Try not to Publish and Forget   145

Section Five - Analyse

Why Analyse?   150

What can we look at?   153

Did our posts perform?   159

Analyse our audience   166

Changes / Improvements   170

Side Topics (Additional Insights)

A breif look at SEO   176

Scaling Campaigns   181

Hashtags   184

Being successful on Instagram   188

Final Thoughts   198

Intro

Mindset of Creating Content

This is all about getting in the mindset for creating content which we can use to promote our businesses.

Our world has become very content driven, it's everywhere we look, our phones, TV, Facebook feeds, billboards and on buses just to name a few.

So what exactly is Content? Well, in short, it's a piece of media produced to promote your business. Whether that be a photo for Instagram, a short video clip for Facebook, a blog article on your website, or a sound bite for a radio ad.

These days to keep up with the competition in all these different media spaces the rate you need to be producing quality content is insane. I've known people say they produce 50 pieces of content a day purely for personal brand accounts.

That sounds crazy but break it down and it becomes very plausible...

- 2 posts on Facebook
- 2 photos on Instagram
- 3 posts on Twitter
- Blog post on own website, that needs thumbnails, content images...
- Then maybe a guest Blog post, same again...
- A handful of Instagram Stories,
- Article for Linked In

That's about 20 pieces of content and that only touches the main outlets. If we started looking at paid Facebook adverts and Adwords campaigns I'm sure we could soon make that double. However, you get my drift. It's deceiving how fast we can get through content and publish it to our audiences.

The only problem with this is that we are always in need of more. More fresh exciting content to create that wow factor and entice our audience to come and spend their money. Posting that same great photo over and over just isn't good enough anymore. It's like someone famous wearing the same great outfit to two Red Carpet events, people notice.

We are a generation seeking out the latest iPhones, Big screen TV and these App Based appliances for our homes. If we want to be reaching out to this audience we need to ensure we are posting new and fresh content and it's these latest iPhones that we all have in our pockets which can be the tools to do the job.

Now don't get me wrong, there is the need for having Professional equipment for high production shoots and yes you can tell the quality difference however we are not there yet. These are high budget operations which we don't need yet, granted the middle ground is currently a good quality Digital SLR camera however for being able to harvest content like a machine, which lets be fair it's sounding like we need to be doing our iPhones or Smart Phones are the perfect tools for the job and challenging to beat for practicality.

Most medium to high-end phones from the past couple of years will have 4K video, Image processing which rivals most digital cameras and have the ability to access that content immediately. This is the kind of tool we never had a few years ago, admittedly the media space wasn't this competitive a few years ago yet that's how things evolve.

So we all have our tools. No need to go out and spend

lots of money just to get the ball rolling, afraid to say that excuse is out the bag. Because we've all done it, wasted loads of money on some really cool piece of kit to do something, played with it for ten minutes, gone 'yeah that's really cool' told everyone down the pub about it and then let it sit and gather dust for all eternity. I know I'm not alone on that one.

So getting in the mindset for creating good content is being able to see opportunity and then seek opportunity. It's about understanding what situations or context can be captured to showcase your business.

I'm going to wind back now to an example where I hadn't been as proactive in creating content and this is where it really hit home to me about the importance of always having this mindset to create content. On a Marketing plan for one of our restaurants was to make a Video. This was to be a short showcase video to basically say wow this is us. Had a narrow window to produce this and at the time I wasn't that phased by this. I had various content already, thinking didn't have to worry about many reshoots, a piece of cake.

Yet that wasn't the case. I did, in fact, have a variety of clips and photos etc...as to be fair I was fairly good at collecting content. Afraid to say I have held customers food up for 20 seconds leaving the kitchen so I can sneak a quick photo. The problem was I had underestimated how much fresh content I, in fact, had at my disposal. So many of the good panning shots of the restaurant being full I had used or were outdated because featured the Jukebox in its old home downstairs.

This was the moment I wished I had been more proactive and really had the mindset for content creation. Seeking out the opportunities for being able to do this and when they'd been a dry spell as it were, create my own.

This is where the so-called 'Insta Hoes' come into their own, they are true content producing machines. I'm being unfair as they are professional influencers however this is a name I hear thrown towards a certain brand of influencers. They're the sort who appear to showcase this insta-famous lifestyle, have brands sponsor them, post a couple of photos and make life look easy. I'll tell you now that's not easy.

These are true entrepreneurs who in most cases created a business out of nothing and have achieved things most of us could only dream of with our businesses.

Note:
These influencers could also be a massive benefit to your business however that's a conversation for another day.

There are two approaches to creating content we can embark on and having a mixture of the two seems to be the best approach.

The first is a structured approach. Now, this does require some forethought and some planning. Naturally, the best approach to Social Media Marketing and Content Marketing is to have a plan. So let's say for example you plan on a rolling 1-month basis. You draw out a framework of what you wish to focus on and promote during this month, taking seasonal holidays and special events or product launches into consideration. From this, you can create a rough list of what content you require in order to fill this plan. A majority of this content you will be able to shoot within a single location and will be mainly photo or video based.

For this, the best method is to book a day or an afternoon aside purely for content creation to tick off most of these required items. A good thing is to try and incorporate other team members who don't normally working on marketing your business. Sometimes fresh-faced ideas can be a real benefit in this process and it's rewarding and possibly good for their job satisfaction to be included in this activity.

So we have our list of shots however it's worth spending the extra time and purposely take a few extra angles. Of the same item. A couple of reasons: In the edit post production you could decide you don't like the lighting or something silly however the main reason is it gives the opportunity to half reuse something.

Let's say for example there's one customer out there who follows you on all social media platforms, Facebook, Twitter, you name it. How about we mix things up a little bit with the photos we use for these posts. Chances are the same message will hit all platforms within a similar time frame. By mixing up the angles of the product we include when scrolling through there brain we stop and think twice. This is because it looks familiar but something different stood out, they scroll back a fraction as to see what it was because their brain didn't register it as the same image they saw most likely two minutes previous on another app. They have that second point of contact with your message and it hints them that second more meaningful time. (Part of the classic 7 points of contact to make a sale).

Simple little tricks like this can be really effective and can be how we seem to burn through so much content so quickly.

Always worth taking the time for extra angles and extras shots. Even a quick panning video clip or taking that step back for a behind the scenes photo or video can provide great content for a blog post where you can take the opportunity to go into more depth and help lure your audience in and engage them in your businesses or brands story and journey. Helps them create that real connection and emotional engagement.

As well as this structured approach the mindset of seeking opportunities comes in and being able to identify these situations on the fly. This is where the benefit of incorporating other team members into the structured photo shoots and marketing activities can really begin to pay off because you naturally can't be everywhere every second of the day within your business to witness these moments and capture this content. This is where mentoring your team also into this mindset of creating content comes into play.

It's about seeing an opportunity to showcase and push a certain product, a special guest happens to casually pop by, a customer purchases a significant item, the team have experimented with something product, something's happening locally, the place is full or something amazing happened. Whatever it is, it's about being in the moment. It's like someone trying to relay something amusing which happened earlier in the day and was one of those situations where it was just funnier at the time or you had to be there.

So we have gone into the mindset of creating content. But what about good content?

We have the process, now we need to simply refine the results.

Finding ways where people can relate to your product, trigger emotion, sense a need for it are positive factors to try and engages.

I have a favourite example and it's not directly in relation to creating content however bare with me. Recently I went with one of the team to a showcase event, would say exhibition but it wasn't, was a small local event held by a health club for its members.

There was a stand selling I believe it was a Banana Ketchup. Now when they did there pitch about this product one of the points was about how great it goes with chips as opposed to regular tomato ketchup. It was great they had some samples however these were in small pots and you are given a spoon to taste with....

This is what stumped us, (Me and chap I was with). Who eats ketchup from a spoon, now I know there will be someone out there however for most of us it goes on burgers or we dip our chips in it and I can't understand why they never brought any chips or dare I say even Doritos. Showcase the product in the manner it's going to be consumed. It's the same way a lot of car manufacturers are getting into lifestyle marketing, especially high-end brands. They take a group of journalists, YouTube etc.. away to some really flash hotel, somewhere hot and treat them to a luxury day out which then get documented as the backdrop to their product or new car being showcased in their content. It creates that element of showcasing more than just the product it's the experience and lifestyle of which that product represents and can bring for you and all I really wanted to know was whether the concept of eating chips in the future would have been completely blown out the window for me by dunking one in this Banana ketchup.

I'll quickly digress again however it's the same reason BMW offers 24 hour test drives on their cars, you take it away, it becomes part of your life and you create that emotional connection with it, you see it as part of your daily life in the hope you'll sign your life away on an expensive PCP agreement.

Finding opportunities to showcase your brand or products in this light within your content creation is where it begins to become really effective content.

For example, if you sell nice watches, photograph them with expensive things, flash cars, boats etc... Often people who go out to buy expensive watches use them as a status symbol and are aspiring for the lifestyle and other items featured in the backdrop of the content. This is where you can start to get a little deeper into the mindset of your audience to pick out these things you can tap into to make that emotional connection.

I always say there are 4 key elements to be taken into consideration with any good marketing campaign. Purpose, Effectiveness, On Brand and Return on investment.

Now if we keep these four things in mind when creating content and planning our marketing strategies for our business we are certainly heading down the right track.

Whether it be when making our own opportunities for content creation, for example, conducting photoshoot days or when seeking opportunities we encounter every day.

Section One

Approach

Don't be a bull in a china shop.

Now I say don't be a bull in a china shop because it is far too easy to rush in and simply think I'm going to take this handful of great photos of my product, post them on Facebook, put some lovely words and everyone is then going to buy them. You could get lucky, however, generally speaking, this isn't reality.

From a proactiveness point of view, fantastic. However, let's say you post these 5 great looking photos:

- How is your potential customer supposed to react when they see these?
- Are you trying to send them somewhere, if so where are you sending them?
- Have you thought when your posting?
- What happens presumably a couple of days later once you've posted all your content?
- Had you thought that far ahead?

Being able to take that step back and be in control of

what you are posting and how you are perceiving its anticipated reaction is key.

Think customer experience and empathises from the customer's point of view. As business owners, it's very easy for your inside experience and knowledge of your products to cloud your judgment when trying to market to customers. In your head without realising you may fill in the blanks in your campaign where unfortunately most of the people you are targeting with your campaigns don't have the ability in which to do that.

Think Call to Action. Map out the anticipated customer journey all the way from first seeing your advert to them giving you money. You could even have some fun and sidetrack yourself by creating a cartoon strip showcasing customer thoughts when seeing your advert, this is digressing, a simple flow chart would suffice to break down the various steps of the process.

Very simple approach

• See Advert for your new Magic Anti Tangle Hair Brush
• Visit Website - 'Still in wonder of its magic abilities'

- Impulse purchase said Magic Hair Brush

By mapping out this process you can understand what you are trying to achieve with the content you are publishing. I understand the example above was a very direct journey to conversion. However, not all pieces of content have this intended purpose. Some may be more subtle, for example how many of you started to picture a cartoon comic strip in your mind a minute ago? It's planting the seed. Sometimes your customers don't even realise they may need or want what you are offering.

Sometimes you have to pitch a scenario and build up to the punch line where you use the content designed for the more direct journey to conversion.

You don't know you need an umbrella until it's raining.

So this is even before you start writing a plan for your content in regards to schedule and type of content. You need to understand what you wish to achieve and how your potential customers will interact with your content. What messages and thoughts do you wish to implant into them which you can tap into through another stage later in your campaign? Very much like what a comedian will often do during a stand-up show.

They engage you through telling a story another great trait of successful marketing campaigns, however during a comedians routine they'll often, about a third of the way into the routine tell a main focal story, digress away to talk about other topics however are able to relate back to the punch line to this main story as part of a later joke to bring that part of the act back to life and reinforce it's presence and purpose. All great things to keep in mind when packaging up thoughts and ideas for your campaigns.

This is also when it's a good time to start thinking about your target audience. Lays the foundation for what type of content you'll produce, language you'll use and this may also alter the engagement with your content and alter the perceived customer experience and journey.

Where are we posting?

This sounds almost a stupid question however when stepping back and assessing your marketing campaign it's a good one to properly outline and determine. It's very easy to be narrow-minded and think Facebook, Facebook, Facebook. Admittedly yes this is very much the king of the Social world with currently over 2 billion monthly active users. That is a staggering reach and does dwarf a lot of its competitors despite the fact YouTube is not far behind Facebook I'm thinking more in the realm of conventional Social Media Sharing platforms which currently has Instagram in the number two spot touching 1 Billion Active monthly users. Still an astronomical reach.

It's fair to say the Big 3 we need to be aiming for are of course the obvious ones, Facebook, Instagram and Twitter. However there are many other platforms becoming increasingly popular and beginning to reach vast audiences, however, some of these newer platforms are grown through trends so being able to safely understand their longevity can be challenging and normally have grown from an initially narrow demographic. This means these can become a great platform to deploy some very clever targeted campaigns with the aim of these pushing viral. Something Coca Cola did with a campaign in Asia with an app called Tik Tok (the music video social app). Not heard of it? Well, Tik Tok was the most downloaded social media app in Q1 2018 and has a greater monthly engagement rate than Snap Chat and Twitter. Crazy! Admittedly is mainly popular amongst the youth in Asia but still, this is a staggeringly fast adoption rate for a social platform. This simply highlights the importance of not dismissing other upcoming platforms and ensuring you are keeping with the trends for assessing where to marketing and post your content.

More mainstream platforms however definitely worth taking advantage of include YouTube, Linked In, Snap Chat and Pinterest.

YouTube

YouTube is the interesting one here as it has grown and developed the influencer marketing space. Its reach is massive and the rate in which content is being uploaded is breathtaking, worth Googling some stats as no doubt whatever I put here will have been super seeded (Currently 300 hours of video content every minute). However, the key is being able to harness this power. How you go about this naturally depends on the type of business you have however it's a creative space for publishing Video User Guides, Product Launch and Demo Videos and Brand Advertising Content. To build brand awareness for your product you could create informative or training videos which hook into and create a use for your product, plants the seed and builds the desire for your product.

This brand advertising content is something where the big retail giants come into their own at Christmas and has become a realm of one up man ship and a competition to see who can create the best Christmas video and customers reveal in excitement anticipating their release.

However, if your subscriber count or reach is let's say still working progress the power of YouTube is that they're already a whole host of brand ambassadors and vloggers out there in which you can reach out to and tailor content with to showcase your product. It's a platform where the possibilities are endless. For example, a very well know You Tuber 'Casey Niestat' works alongside Samsung and does some fantastic product collaboration videos with them and showcases the power of their new mobile devices as a content creating tool. It creates that aspirational emotional connection to what that device is capable of and is something which is accessible empowering you to believe you can go out and do the same, which you can!

Linked In

Linked In is another very well established platform however is very much a business networking orientated platform heavily used by recruiters as their golden gem resource however is a lot of organic usage where professional as well as basically itemising a CV as a profile page can share achievements and articles. These articles are a great way for professionals to showcase themselves through personal branding and marketing, typically used by freelancers to create business and attract clients. Along with personal achievements and posts, businesses can directly post company updates and news.

Snap Chat

Snap Chat is on a little bit of a wave currently, It grew massively originally, however, was never commercialised until it had a user base. What's really put Snap Chat on the map is it's 'Snap Chat Filters' For those out of touch this is where your children's puppy ears originate from. Now Snap Chat is commercialised there are some unique ways in which you can tap into it. The expensive way is you can in-fact develop your own branded Snap Chat Filters however I would suggest having deep pockets or a very well targeted campaign before embarking down this route though as cool as it may be. The most accessible way to tap into the platforms commercial aspect is through its geotagging. This is where users can swipe and put a location stamp on their photos and you can design and publish your own for use in certain locations. Something I have previously run campaigns with targeting students during freshers week for venue brand awareness. Of course, the other more conventional method is to make use of this as the social photo sharing platform it was originally designed to be and use for sharing content and adding to your Snap Chat story for your audience to see.

Pinterest

Pinterest, in essence, is link sharing your favourites or bookmarked list of your web browser. It's a publicly pinned social networking pinboard with the original scope of allowing users to connect through their interests in similar content. Reflecting on this concept in some ways I don't understand why there is not a search history based dating app, however, could be a step far. Pinterest is a creative place to be able to showcase your content, and Pin articles of interest which relate to your business or interests of your niche luring them in towards your brand. An interesting demographic fact is that around 80% of Pinterest users are women.

Blogging

Is a classic however still, to be honest, a personal favourite. Having a blog on your company website offers a range of benefits and is often dismissed or overlooked by many small to medium-sized businesses. However I feel this is one of your biggest assets for communicating with your customers and its a platform in which content creates content because through the process of writing an article for your own site you are in turn creating a piece of content which you can share directly on to your social media platforms and drive your audience closer to your business and onto your site. Not only is it a great way to Communicate with customers and be able to offer more information than you can squeeze into a tweet, but it also aids in your sites SEO and helps improve your search engine rankings. This is because the search engines see your site is regularly maintained and updated with new informative content being published.

There are different ways you can use your blog. You could choose to treat your blog as a company news outlet and purely publish new products, business developments etc...This is great for those following your business however has a very corporate feel and doesn't really attract or engage a wide audience. One way you could use your businesses blog is to offer insight into topics relating to your product, service or industry and treat as a real marketing tool to lure visitors to your brand / business and try to convert them into customers. A company which offers social media posting tools could blog about current trends and stats around various platform usage, (seemed a very on brand example). This offers value to potential customers and builds their trust and relationship with your brand and increases the likely hood of you to convert these into actual paying customers.

Note:
Another angle worth considering is platforms like 'medium.com' where you can share your blog posts from your website with a larger audience.

The Big 3

Of course not forgetting the Big 3, Facebook, Instagram and Twitter. Most of these have now evolved to a point where you have new ways in which you can post. Mimicking Snap Chat, Facebook and Instagram have launched their own Stories feature over the past couple of years. Of course with Facebook owning Instagram you can post on one and directly share to the other which can prove useful. The powerful one here is Instagram's which I feel really shuck Snap Chat and has made this feature into a commercial product with great ways to reach and engage an audience.

The stories feature is a great way to directly engage with your audiences on top of regularly posted content and allows a great platform for Live updates and storytelling for that personal interaction and connection. One great use example is by hosting a poll through your Instagram story and get quick fire market research feedback from your audience. This is a power which took a small army to plan and implement successfully in yesteryear however with a few taps we can harvest this kind of information almost instantaneously.

Twitter being a microblogging platform pretty much

invented the hashtag for users to openly classify and categories content. This makes Twitter a great platform to host a discussion regarding live events. Ever spotted many TV shows even promote their own Hashtags, this is the reason. They can create viral content and discussions live, which in turn notify users and lure them into watching so they can intern be part of the conversation.

I've not touched heavily on the Big 3 at this stage as how these each can be used will be put into practice later in the book.

Where are we sending our customers?

So we have established where we can post our content. So the next stepping stone would in theory be the content it self. However we are going to brush over that part for now and think what we want from our customers and how we wish them to interact.

By understanding how we want our customers to react to our content and how we envisage them taking their next step in their potential customer journey gives us the power to refine our content to encourage this perceived outcome.

Different types of content naturally dictate different routes for our customers to follow. Again the type of business you are will also determine where you are sending your customers as the point of conversion will have a different location, may it be digital or physical.

Let's say your a fashion brand and you post some content to social media which has a photo of someone wearing one of your outfits in some cool lifestyle like image. The natural thought here would be quick send them to the shopping cart and have their money. Hasty I know but this is business, we all think like this. Yes the direct route in this case would often make a lot of sense, it minimises the steps your potential customer is required to convert in to a sale. A lot of times fashion can be an impulse purchase so it would make sense to simplify our funnel here to capitalise of this trait.

There was such a thing amongst web designers as the unofficial 3 click rule. This was the rule of thumb that when a user visits your website they should have to use no more than 3 mouse clicks in order to find the information they're looking for. The three clicks was based on the belief that beyond this users of a site will become frustrated, lose interest and leave.

This infact makes perfect sense and is a great mentality to adopt and include in our marketing practises and when we are mapping out our prospective customer journeys in order to improve conversion rates.

Instead of linking directly to your product page you could link to a blog post or article and create more of a emphasis around what it means to be wearing your fashion brand and lure prospective customers into the lifestyle and make them feel emotionally obligated to buy your products...

This adds another step in the journey however could be a way to ensure your prospective customers stay on the right path.

It's always something worth taking the step back to consider and evaluate. It's about forecasting at what point of their journey your prospective customers are and choosing the manor of approach to best ensure conversion.

One mindset to help you choose the best approach is referring to this process as Fishing. First piece of content wows them and hooks them in. After that you need to simply reel them in so you can bag them in your net, however the size of the fish (or scale of purchase) could affect how long and how much effort is required to successfully catch them. For bigger fishes just letting them go a little and teasing them (with more content) will weaken them making it gradually easier to reel them in and catch them.

It maybe a case you're trying to promote a product

which would be regarded as an impulse purchase thus a well timed post or advert to quickly whisk them through the checkout would be the chosen route. For example if you are trying to sell a cheap pancake frying pan on the run up to Pancake Day you want to catch the customer while that impulse is hot and get the transaction completed before they have chance to think otherwise, or remember theres one in the cupboard which they purchased the previous year.

You may have a full campaign mapped out designed to lure customers to a larger purchase or commitment. This is something which more rationale would be involved within the decision making process. This is where playing the longer game and linking to more informative content and creating a mix of content to portray the bigger picture lure and showcase the benefits of making this purchase or choice come into play. This is where you design a campaign around building trust and brand engagement and harbour back to the traditional 7 Points of Marketing.

You maybe able to convert this customer within this interaction. You may have to let them go and get them on another visit. However if we've been able to get that initial hook and are playing the long game it's worth then trying to find an angle to at least grab a hold on them. If we've sent our audience to other

content being that either a blog post or a landing page of some sorts, it's worth dangling some bait towards obtaining another source of interaction with them. Having a prominent offer or deal wrapped around collecting an email address to add to a tailored mailing list for re-marketing at a later date.
From here you can then link from your email campaigns back to other blog content etc...or send them direct to purchase.

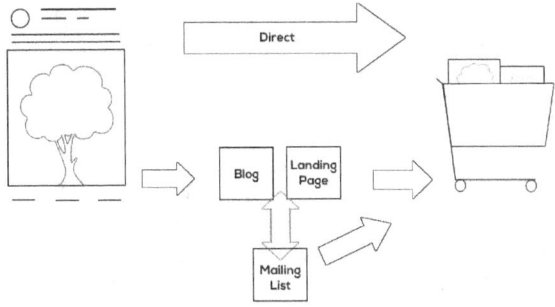

Note:
Other remarketing opportunities arise if you have Facebook tracking pixels setup correctly within your website. You can then create campaigns to retarget these users at a later date with the scope of then converting them.

What can we achieve?

So we've looked at:
- Where we can post
- Where we can send customers

Now to look at what we can achieve. When looking at where we can send our customers we were focusing directly on converting into sales and the funnel in which we can use to achieve this.

The simple starting point here is goals. We need to take the thinking from the previous two thought processes and start reiterating that into tangible milestones and goals for our business. Sounds simple however financial gain or sales isn't necessarily the only thing we can measure here to define a goal.

There is in-fact a whole host of different things we can look to achieve, These can be considered as building blocks towards that end result of a sale. Each of these building blocks can serve a different purpose and some of which can be used to aid in you converting other members of your audience.

Below I'm basically going to list a variety of things we can put goals towards and measure through our social media campaigns.

• Overall Product sales.

• Specific Product sales, maybe a new line, a seasonable special etc...

Note:
When measuring against product sales we could take the total number of sales as a whole or if have a variety of traffic sources it could be worth effectively setting up Google Analytics (Loads of YouTube Videos) to track conversions and then can break down and analyse conversions from specific traffic sources.

• Mailing list subscribers. This is an underrated asset within most businesses, the power of building a real targetable mailing list is invaluable. Email Marketing is a completely different avenue in which we can publish our content to engage our audience. It's a very direct approach and we can really hone in on the analytics and understand exactly who has opened our content and clicked through to the next part of the journey.

• Claim a voucher, whether it be for a physical or digital purchase this is a solid stepping stone here. We can also use this as a gateway to collect data for an email campaign and build our mailing list.

• Build Brand awareness through engagement. This is when you don't necessarily wish to send your audience on to another step, you want to trigger a conversation and use them to help push your content and brand viral to help put your brand logo and name in front of as many people as possible. Now naturally it's hard to guarantee who these posts may reach however most platforms have the ability to see where it went through tracking engagement.

• Improve public image and perception. This is through building customer reviews and ratings. Unfortunately, it is unethical to incentivise customers to leave a positive review however to encourage them to leave honest feedback is perfectly acceptable.

There was once a story I came across someone who

worked in a restaurant which was incentivising its staff to get mentions in good Trip Advisor reviews. The anticipated organic way of achieving this would be through excellent customer engagement and service however this member of staff was rather crafty. The incentive was £10 bonus for every mention, seems fair however what they did was sit down with the customers and offer them a £5 cut to post a review mentioning them during their meal and simply hand them £5 cash which usually worked it's way back around in form of a tip. Unfortunately, this member of staff appeared too good at this and was eventually caught out.

Note:
If you were going to try and implement this slightly devious method, from experience have received negative backlash from Trip Advisor stating that reviews were all coming from the same location so were perceived as fake. These all were, in fact, honest and ethically obtained reviews however guests were all making use of our Free Wifi and this was causing some confusion. Despite arguing the case we never won, just a side note worth considering.

These here are just a couple of suggestions of thing you can achieve and measure through social media. Another great one is something which would cross-reference a little here with brand awareness on certain platforms would be using social media to obtain Market Research data. To gain feedback on your products, obtain input for business decision making through social media tools such as being able to hold Polls with your audience is powerful and could be something worth keeping in mind for potential content when putting together our content for our schedules later on, is a great one for pushing more viral through means of interaction, two birds with one stone.

Now I'm curious here as to whether the obvious thing we can achieve here has crossed your mind. It's one thing which is inherently simple to measure and keep track of. This is, of course, growing our audience. This is something in which we would be able to hopefully achieve organically through setting and seeking some of the above goals with the use of good Content. This is one of the key things in which businesses seek to achieve with social media and is something which is easy to get hung up on. The larger audience simply means more fish in the pond to take your bait in the first place.

We can also use our social platforms to leverage and influence followers towards one another. I won't lie is something I hate to see overused from a personal perspective however from a business continuity aspect is a no brainer. Let say heaven forbid and suddenly overnight Facebook goes down or on a smaller scale your page gets hacked and blocked. If this was your sole or prime social media platform its fair to say in this instance you'd be slightly screwed, so always worth keeping in mind and could be something to occasionally cross-reference within your social media plan.

A great way would be to hook into types on content or abilities that each social media platform specialises in and makes the user feel like they have to follow on this other platform for unique content. How you do this will differ between businesses however easy example is Push the Stories aspect on Instagram, and live conversation on Twitter with 'x' hashtag. Find an angle to make use of the strengths and USP's of each platform.

Type of Content we can Create

This sounds like an obvious one however beyond the basics and more common types of content each platform has its own new ways you can package content and display it to your audience, some of which however are tailored towards paid promotions and work more effectively on different platforms.

- Plain text
- Photo
- Panoramic / 3D Photos
- Video
- Polls
- Shared Articles
- Posts or Stories

We could keep our posts simple. Go with just plain text. This is something which can work better on Twitter compared to others purely because it's the medium in which the platform was originally founded. Twitter was always designed as a microblogging site and was focused around broadcasting short, sweet updates. It then broadened to photos and video content to compete with features of competition, not a bad thing. For a quick short and sweet status update to your audience or a short informative message, plain text pretty much does the job.

Photos help enrich our content and harbours back to the old saying of 'A picture tells the story of a thousand words'. The key to ensuring the story in which our photo is trying to tell is on message with what we are aiming to achieve.

The same goes for video content. This is the next elevation of content and the song which has come to mind as I type this is 'Video Killed the Radio Star'. Video content is the current pinnacle of medium for storytelling and I don't know of a classic saying here, however hard to deny a 'Video tells the story of a Million words'.

A photo is a great way of grabbing someone's attention and a video is a great way of holding on to it. It's about getting the balance of content to publish with our message and to effectively and efficiently deliver it.

However how we frame our shots and how we focus on our brand or product can help us deliver and emphasis our messages differently. Below are a few key examples where I have used a bottle of Wine as the product:

Contextual:
Great for demonstrating a real-world situation which your product can enrich or used for identifying and showing off a specific USP of your Product.

Post: Guest coming round? Crack open Le Plonk...

Hero:
Perfect for when you want to solely focus on the product its self.

Post: Have you tried our 'Bottle Le Plonk'? Refreshingly light fruity taste.

Close Up:
Ideal for focusing on a specific detail.

Post: 2017 was a great year for growing on our vineyard.

Obscure:
For when you wish to create a situation where your brand image isn't specifically in the foreground or the main focus of the image.

Post: Long day.....why not unwind with a cheeky glass or two...

Key is when planning your content to get a balance of these types of images to both showcase and tell an enticing story, to build the desire for your brand or product.

Another good example could involve a bag company. We could have a 'Hero Shot' photo of a new bag, this would focus attention and clearly display the new product (a backpack in this case). Maybe there's a special pocket to quickly access your passport, a 'Close Up' shot of someone sliding there passport out would emphasise this USP. We could then create a scenario where we have a plane parked at the gate with passenger boarding. The photo is then of the passenger at the top of the steps boarding and shot in a way where we can see the bag and the bag's design allows the brand to clearly be seen and identified. This showcases the bag in a 'Contextual' shot and portrays a scenario in our prospective customer's mind where they can see themselves in and relate to. Making them feel inclined to purchase the product for their next trip.

Understanding how you can use these different types of shots can give your fantastic food for thought when dreaming up content ideas and even trying to take a structured approach to market and showcase your product and create content. With the Bag example above you could take a series of Hero Shots to go with a variety of messages, a Variety of shots of people using them, whether be packing or travelling to exotic locations for the Contextual Angle. You can then break down a list of all the key features and think of creative ways to show these off in a range of Close Up or Contextual. Then in regards to the obscure, this is where you have a very blank canvas to showcase creativity and personally I find these can prove very effective pieces of content, there more subtle and can almost gear themselves towards more of a lifestyle marketing approach. You could do a photo along check-in line (framed waist down towards the desk), here you could then have a couple of your branded bags tucked in amongst the queue. This could be great for an engagement post with the message of 'Don't you just hate Check-In Queues? Where was your worst experience?' And create a conversation about a situation your product is nearly in the background of.

These same approaches can be upscaled to video content as well however I'm sure you can appreciate that from an example point of view photos are way easier to talk about.

There is always the opportunity to not directly make your own content. There are thousands of Stock Images out there which would no doubt apply to your industry. However, if your product is very distinctive or brand orientated your own content may prove way more effective.

However, you may not be wishing to post any of your own content. You may have come across a

'Contextual' style Article which fits alongside your brand and would add benefit to your audience. These can be a great way to add valuable content to your feeds with little effort. I will mention, Don't take the opportunity to be the Bull in a China shop here...take a moment and see if could think of an enchanting tagline to share the Article on your page with, this is where you can personalise the content and probe user engagement with the post and your page. This is the sort of thing which works great on Facebook and Twitter however Instagram kinda lacks its capacity in this merit, which is fair.

A type of content becoming ever so more popular is the use of 'Stories' Feature on platforms such as Instagram. It offers the ability for storytelling and helps engage a wide audience on a very personal level. With limited availability of this content because it naturally fades off your story feed after a period of 24 hours it's great for maintaining constant engagement and even testing the engagement level of your audience. As a side or more regular feature to your regular posting its a very powerful addition. It can naturally play home for very off the cuff and impromptu content however is worth thinking of content you can feature as a planned story.

Let's say you're a restaurant who offers takeaway on

deserts. Many guests might not be aware of this feature. You could create a story to showcase them from a first-person perspective:

- Sitting down for their meal.
- Looking at the time.
- Having a carryout bag (branded) Infront of them
- A cheeky nose inside (overlay text, did you know we do takeaway?)
- A shot of them walking out the door, bag swinging into view
- Sat on sofa tucking in.

This tells a story which any of your customers could replay themselves and showcases a key feature(s), in this instance, amazing deserts and the main thing, the ability to take them home with you.

This would be a great example to implement as planned content and is something you can use to showcase any USP's your business offers.

You could go one step beyond using the stories feature and simply go LIVE. This is a feature which all of the 'Big 3' offer and is a very raw approach however if well planned can prove very effective. These social platforms are geared towards actively pushing live content and are able to use Push Notifications to give your audience a nudge and tell them you're live and beckon them to come see. It offers direct interaction with your audience as they can message you in real time and you can respond back live. Is a really powerful tool which is currently very underutilised within many businesses however an area of social media which I can see evolving a lot more over the coming few years.

Benefits of Blogging

Blogging is very quickly becoming a very powerful content marketing tool for businesses and they're still many businesses out there who underutilise this medium.

Originally it was something I felt very hesitant about embarking with using within my own businesses however began including a putting together a basic blog within business websites purely from an SEO standpoint. Having a blog is actually seen as a rateable factor with many major search engines and they'll keep track of whether you are keeping the content up to date. Search Engines love fishing for current and relevant content meaning blogging can be a fantastic way to boost your websites rankings and to attract new users to your brand.

They're different ways in which you can structure your business blog. You could treat it as a news / information platform to inform your audience of changes and things going on within your business. It allows loyal followers of your blog to become emotionally engaged and connected with your business and build a relationship with them. It's almost like following a radio Presenter, by listening to them regularly, more often than not on a daily basis you begin to feel like you know them as a person and more familiar with them than some members of your friendship group because of this consistent interaction. Blogs can serve this same purpose.

Having this catalogue of content available to read on your website also allows new users to play catchup and binge on your block like they would a box set on Netflix if they felt a connection.

Other ways in which you could use your blog in to lure customers to your brand. You may wish to use your blog as a way to showcase how your product can be used and portray the greater benefits of it almost from a case study point of view to entice users.

You may be a car manufacturer or dealer and you could put together travel content or lifestyle content focused around the car and the journey. Create and design content around ideas which your audience can aspire or relate to. A road trip highlighting great points of interest along a route as a great way to spend a long weekend with the core focal engine of this adventure being the car. Or you could do something along the lines of going to a family party, some silly stories of drunk aunty Sandra's escapades but the focus is the journey, picking of key features along the way, the sat—nav rerouting around traffic around Nottingham, the rear charging point because you forgot to charge the kids iPads. Silly little things which you can build a story around.

It's a platform in which you can personify your brand and products or create a valuable pool of content to help attract customer to your business. It's also a two birds one stone kind of outlet as by formulating a blog post with rich content for your website you are very much intern creating quality content which you can publish on your social media platforms.

Section Two

Plan

What are we Promoting?

The last thing to take into consideration before we can properly put pen to paper is to think about what we are promoting. Sounds almost obvious however depending what exactly we are promoting or our type of business can alter our approach slightly. With different types of products comes slightly different focal points which are worth keeping fresh in our mind as we embark on the following stages.

The spectrum here is vast so to offer food for thought I'm going to simply note a few key examples. These should touch upon a few key points to note and help you take on the mindset to assess your own products etc... in this manner.

Events:
- When advertising events, you have to keep in mind the time aspect.
- Dependant on the scale of the event are you offering enough lead time in order to promote it? (Too early though it may not be fresh in the thoughts

of your audience)
- Keep in mind the event date?
- Any other big events or similar events on around the same time (could you find an angle of leveraging them into your campaigns?)
- Do you require prior commitment from guests attending, ticket sales, bookings etc? How are you diverting traffic from your posts to support this?
- Chances are you would have used the Events feature in Facebook, are you diverting traffic from other social platforms here or are you diverting all event-related traffic to your website or a 3rd party source to register commitment?

Product:
- Is this a physical or digital product?
- Are you sending your audience to a physical location to purchase or online (consider operational/opening hours)
- If purchasing from a physical location, are these locations limited?
- Would this be considered an impulse purchase?
- Is there a special offer with a. Time restriction related to this product?

Is it a Product Launch?:
- How can we build hype?
- Do we send to a mailing list or to one of our other

social platforms to be first to hear more details?
(Excuse to build other social/marketing platforms)
- Keep launch date in mind.
- As well as all aspects relating to normal products.

Service (physical or digital?):
- How are you delivering this service?
- How are customers engaging to apply or receive this service?
- Is it a one off or recurring?

These are questions to be asking yourself so key points are fresh in your mind. Of course when thinking about what you are promoting you always have to consider your audience and target audience. How are they perceiving this content, interacting, how and when? Thinking through these things upfront allows you to consistently flow through the following stages and consider the new questions you'll need to be asking yourself in order to produce an effective content plan.

How often are we posting?

This is where our plan begins to start physically taking form and we can get hands on. Out there is a variety of different tools for doing this and even scheduling your content. In regards to this we are going to visually map out using good old fashioned Pen and Paper, sometimes it's a hard medium to beat. However in regards to online tools, at the point of writing this, I would recommend 'Planable'. I've tried a few and it has the best calendar-based planning facility when compared to others on the market. (It's useful, but don't jump to search for it straight away)

We need to think about how often we want to be touching base with our audience. It's about getting the fine balance of keeping them informed without spamming them and them choosing to stop following you. One way we can look at trying to post more and keep users positively engaged is through storytelling, they become engaged and eagerly awaiting the next part of the tail to unfold through your next post, this is social media goals right here.

We need to think of your demographic. It naturally makes life easier when targeting a single timezone because the time of day based posts can become very effective and it can be easier to judge when your audience is likely to be absorbing content through their devices.

So for an example let's say we are targeting a UK office based audience and one window where users will kick back and look at their phones for example or have a cheeky scroll through Facebook at their desk would be during Lunch. It's safe to say our window here is between 12 and 2. My personal approach here would be to post 11:47 am with something strong and engaging. This is because you have the window for some early engagement to help the content gain traction and support its relevance to help the powers of the social algorithms push it out to your wider audience by the time a majority of them come online early lunch.

Types of content great for pushing here is something which could alter actions for that evening. Let's say you're a takeaway, this would be a prime opportunity to target your audience with a midweek special offer because this would be the time when people could be texting their partners going ' Hey Hun, fancy curry later? The Spice Yard has 20% Off', Boom. It's breaking into the phycology and actions of your audience and getting into their mindset and looking at key opportunities to hack into it.

Getting into this mindset and pick a time slot or two a day where we can target our audience gives us a great opportunity to feed them content. It can come across as more acceptable to post multiple times on different platforms, for example, Twitter is a good place for short regular tweets and is a great space for interacting with other users to help grow your audience and start a conversation. It may be a case as on most platforms you aim to post daily with on some days supplementary posts to either reinforce the same message or to tackle and broadcast a message relating to another theme.

In the previous chapter, we outlined the platforms we are wishing to post content on, the Big 3 (Facebook, Twitter, Instagram). From here we can create our proposed schedules, now it's worth bearing in mind we may choose to vary times for better targeting at a later stage when we marry our schedules with our content however this offers a fantastic foundation framework.

I stated that we were going to go back to old school

Pen and Paper for this, means low battery can't be used as an excuse to procrastinate here. If we take a sheet of A4 paper for each social media platform we can list the days of the week across the top. If you're like me you could even fold the page and work from A5 size is a habit of mine as easier to pin under the front of my Mac when typing from notes. So now we have our days we can build one week at a time, let's walk before we run.

If you've started with Monday let's think when you're starting from and put a date against it. This allows you to incorporate and circle special days like valentines or pancake day.

Under these days we can draw a box for each time slot we wish to add (bear in mind we shall draw a line and put the following week below)

At the top of each box, state the proposed post time and leave space for us to reference content to post, (space for a big number 77, for example, will do the job).

Let's draw a line, in the columns aligned with the days of the week, make a quick note of the calendar day

(22nd for eg) and let's repeat this process until we have around a month's worth of days covered. This now gives a visual of the number of pieces of content we need to produce. It's deceiving how quickly it can escalate however in the next section we'll tackle how to become very efficient at producing content so it doesn't completely take over your life.

This is a good opportunity to scan over your schedule and make sure you have an even spread in regards to time slots. Ensure you have repeated this process for each of our social media platforms and cross-reference constancy amongst these.

Your core time slots you want to make fairly consistent across the board purely because let's say you choose later on to drop in content for a grand announcement, It would kind of lose its magic if it hit one platform considerably earlier than another. Have to think about the end result and from an end users point of view of absorbing the message.

Those platforms where you have scheduled a number of extra time slots it's worth marking these. A good system is by the time stamp in the boxes if it's a completely unique posting slot then mark with a single Asterix or Star if crosses two platforms with this time slot 2 Stars and then if consistent across the board leave blank. This creates a counting system and elevates too much effort if posting everywhere at the same time.

This now gives a set of blank calendars as it were with our slots from dropping in our content. This is treated as a starter for ten, purely because as mentioned earlier when dropping in our final content we may find it more effective to alter a posting time slightly.

Below is an example of how your schedule could look:

Note:
In the examples I have only covered general content posting and a 3 week period, however, you get the gist of it. You will spot a couple of variations between each platform where I have altered the schedules.

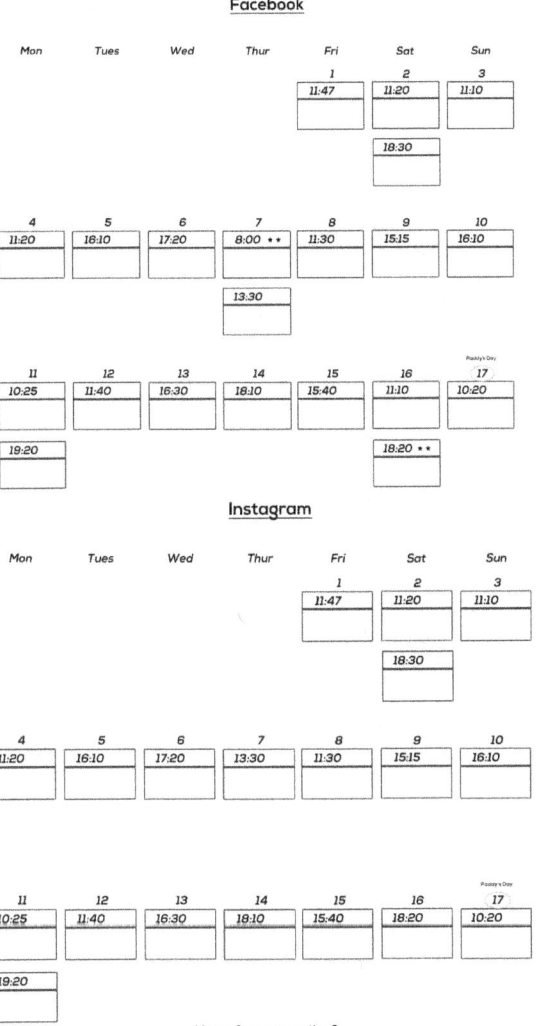

How often are posting?

Twitter

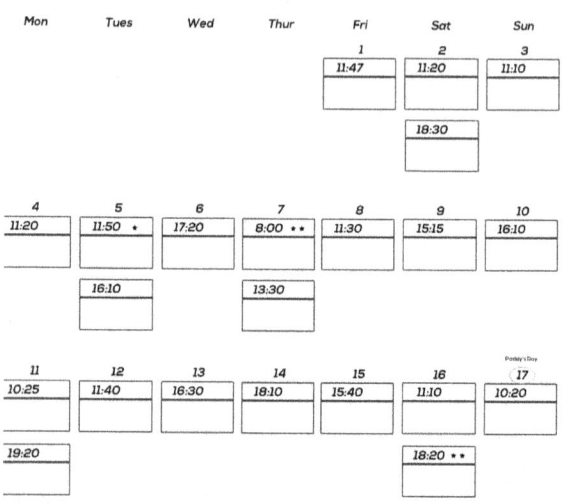

Section Two | Plan

Choosing our Themes

When talking about themes I'm referring to the category of content we wish to publish. These could be broad themes or rather specific. One broad example could be a brand value or USP in which we wish to enforce. Something along the lines of 'A guaranteed service response time'.

More specific themes could be in relation to a specific event or a gig in which you are promoting, here you can focus upon the journey leading up to the event. For example, the content you could build around this theme could be along the lines of:

- The announcement of Event Coming soon
- Tickets going on sale 'X' date
- Tickets now on sale, grab your's while you can
- Teaser of Event content
- Early doors tickets now Sold Out, grab yours while you can
- 2nd Teaser of Event content
- Ticket Giveaway Competition

- Don't forget, 'X' date this Event is happening
- Countdown to Event and Final Tickets
- Today this Event - Some public information about where to go
- Flashback and thanking those who attended.

Here you can see how you can easily map out a series of content opportunities relating to a theme. Through taking a structured approach as here in a chronological sense it can be easier to build the bigger picture and churn out a series of content. This example could potentially be a theme, dependant upon lead-time of promoting the event, a Content Theme which could span a couple of months.

Think about your business and what are the key things that come to mind you wish to showcase on social media?

Is there any key dates coming up which you circled on your Posting Schedule, whether it be specific to your business or a national holiday or day in which you can jump on to as a marketing opportunity.

#NationalYoYoDay - No ups and down's with us, consistent customer service you can rely on.

Cheesy cheap shot I know however there is always an angle to be creative and I don't even know whether national YoYo day is even a thing. Pancake Day, for example, you could arrange for some of your team to make pancakes for lunch as a team building activity, this is something which you could aim to showcase and capitalise from the opportunity from.

There are better ones to aim for and national well known holidays such as Mothers Day are key ones to target and build content around, as of course Christmas.

Note:
Take time to think of national holidays of events celebrated within other cultures. Is there an opportunity regarding any of those. I'm not saying jump on every single one. However globally we are becoming a very multicultural society and within your audience or demographic there may be a few key ones worth highlighting.

By choosing a theme it creates a form of consistency with your posting and allows an opportunity to reinforce a message through a series of posts or to find a way to build a story around it to lure people into through multiple pieces of content to sell a greater message.

Lets keep it simple and choose 4 keys themes for example (I would normally say choose between 3 and 7, again something which depends on your business and what's going on, however choosing too many your audience will simply lose track of what's going on and you will blow their mind, not necessarily in a good way.

For this example we shall go with 4 simple themes:

1. Brand
2. Product 1
3. Sale Event
4. Product 2

These will be elaborated on further in the following chapter when we build from this our post content. To add context to this we are going to say we are a Burger Bar and have a terrible name such as 'Big Burgers' because for this is irrelevant.

- Our Brand Values will be around using only the freshest locally sourced ingredients to ensure the highest quality produce.

- Product 1 can be our Three Cheese Big Beefy (three slices of cheese, 3 thick patties)
- Sale Event can be a new lunchtime offer, any main 'Big Burger' meal for £3 (With Voucher)
- Product 2 can be our new Vegan Burger 'The Unbeeflevable'

Making a List of Messages

This is where we get to elaborate from our themes we have just mapped out and my poorly named Burger Bar 'Big Burger' shall come to life and potentially have you craving burgers by the end of the chapter, sorry my bad.

It's key to remember here that we have different platforms in which we may wish to broadcast the same message. The aim is to be as consistent with the message as possible however leveraging and adhering to how the specific platform formats in which we are publishing on.

Again this is where we can take out the trusty Pen and Paper and up one side we can list our themes with the scope of branching out from these into a spider diagram where we can list our potential messages and even list them in a story format as I did with the Event example in the previous chapter.

With our messages we need to ensure we focus on the point at hand, get our message across and make them easy to read. With Facebook especially there's the opportunity to format your post cleanly with use of emoji and breaking content over multiple lines. This allows us to tailor the post to be eye-catching, engaging and informative all in one and really embrace our potential client.

We need to consider the use of pictures and whether to include links to external content, this depends on the desired result of the post. Going back to Section One of this book it's considering whether we are looking to funnel traffic, build brand engagement or plant a seed.

Note:
When including links it could be worth making a short link (Google 'short link' for a site to create these). With short links, we can keep our posts looking sleek and also keep track of click-throughs to measure the campaign results.

Below I have created 5 example posts for each of the 4 Themes. These soon quickly add up to be 20 pieces of content. These will by default be worded / produced for Facebook however with one example from each Theme I shall reword an example for Twitter and Instagram. The inclusion of HashTags will be very basic purely because these are constantly evolving. (See back of the book to learn more about the use of Hashtags)

Brand Values
Using only the freshest locally sourced ingredients to ensure the highest quality produce.

All of the beef in our burgers is ground on site and is sourced locally from "Fred's Butchers"

Big Burger Instagram
All of the beef in our burgers is ground on site and is sourced locally from @redbull #local

Never Frozen. Thats what gives the sizzle....

Odds are you traveled further than our ingredients

Making a List of Messages

Note:
When I created the first post I tagged the Butchers on each of the different profiles. It's worth noting if using a 3rd party posting tool or just copying and pasting your text these tags don't always work. Worth checking them before posting.

Product 1
Our Three Cheese Beefy (three cheeses, 3 thick patties)

Big Burger
3 mighty patties, layered with cheese...
Have you tried the Three Cheese Beefy?

Big Burger
Once, twice, three times a Beefy

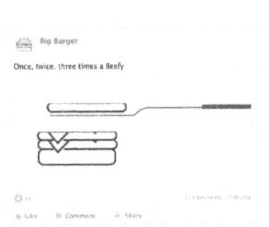

Big Burger
Have you thought about dinner yet?

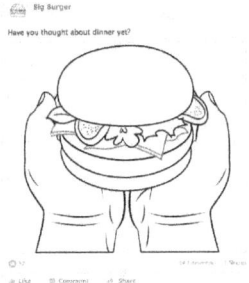

Making a List of Messages

Note:
Begin thinking of the ordering of posts or the times of day in which you could post this content. When pushing a product a Hero Shot is a great solid post for introduction. It means when posting more diverse content regarding that product a majority of your audience should hopefully have some familiarity with it and will naturally associate.

Sale Event

Lunch time offer of any main 'Big Burger' meal for £3 (With Voucher)

Big Burger

🍔 Want your Big Burger Lunch meal for Only £3?
👉 Download your vouchers here: billy.co/6hhbjknk

Big Burger

🍔 Hump Day Blues?
🍔 Why not £3 Moo's?
🍔 All our meals £3 at lunch with voucher!
👉 Grab yours now....billy.co/6hhbjknk

Big Burger

Maybe theres a better option?

Making your Lunch can be a Chore

Note:

It's worth thinking about the 'time of day' for when publishing the 3rd post here regarding a packed lunch alternative. This could be a good post for an evening when people are trying to find the motivation to leave the sofa and undertake this task. Emotionally tap into their thought process.

You may also notice in the Instagram post it's a paid advert. This is because Instagram doesn't allow links in descriptions, other ways around this are stating 'link in bio' or if qualified, use link in story or Instagram shopping features.

Product 2
Our new Vegan Burger 'The Unbeeflevable'

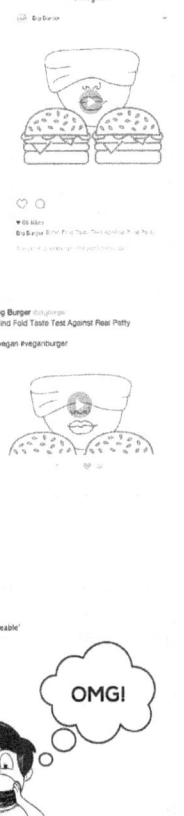

Big Burger
Blind Fold Taste Test Against Real Patty

Big Burger
The NEW: The Unbeeflevable
100% Vegan Friendly Burger which tastes well....Like real meat!

Big Burger
Blind Fold Taste Test Against Real Patty
#vegan #veganburger

Big Burger
That tastes 'udderliveable'

OMG!

The Unbeeflevable

Making a List of Messages

Note:

When posting video content to Instagram, take into consideration the length of video you can post. (Currently capped at 60 seconds). If you have longer content it may be worth using the Instagram Stories feature and then featuring your Content on your page or Instagram TV (a new feature)

With all of these, you can see that I have followed the key points of each represented theme and included images with most posts of which the scope can clearly represent the individual message. It allows the image to reiterate what your words are speaking ensuring your message is portrayed to the best of its ability.

It's good practice to pick on messages for each theme which will pull on an emotional string of engagement with your end user. This doesn't have to be something deep and sad however with the first example of 'Locally sourced meat' and including the local butchers tagged in the post. The locally sourced element is something a lot of people feel strongly about and is one way which not only can you source quality ingredients, lower your carbon footprint and all of that glorious stuff it's a way you can reach out to your customers and pull on their feelings and beliefs. It reaches them on that emotional level. By naming and tagging the local butcher in this case it creates part of a story in which your audience can relate to. In respect to this business, chances are we are reaching out to predominately a local audience and they may be familiar with our supplier or have seen one of their vans on the roads. It helps build the engagement into the narrative.

This tagging of your supplier in your post also opens

the door for a cross promotion. There's not a competitor and may have a really good reputation in the area. It's something to show off from your perspective, it offers them some publicity and hopefully, it can become a mutual marketing collaboration and they can either repost your content or create there own including your business as the focal point. Allows you to reach out to their audience as well as your own.

As you can see some of these examples are slight tongue and cheeky however demonstrate ways in which we can build our content around our given themes to create engaging messages.

You can see the varied use of emojis amongst these. Those with emojis are a lot cleaner to read. It's about balancing the use of them, littering your post with them just looks messy however using them a decorative bullet point almost can prove very effective and allows our brains to summaries the text before we've read it.

When creating your spider diagrams with your messages it's worth making a tally of the number of boxes you created in your Posting Schedule. This is to ensure you are creating enough content in which to fill them. Some platforms such as Twitter may require extra messages creating to complete the schedule, is good to keep note of.

Below is a spider diagram example of how you can draft build up your lists of messages for each theme.

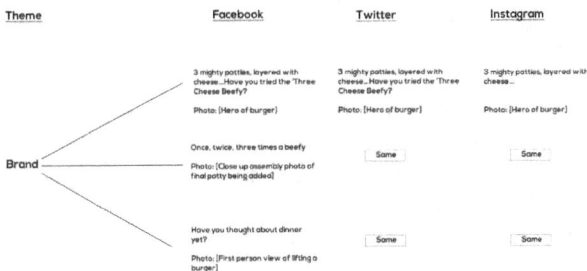

Note:
I have simply put descriptions for the type and content of the images associated with each message.

Consideration of Paid Campaigns and Specific Targeting

Are we going to be using any of our content for paid campaigns and specific targeting?

This is an important thing to consider when looking at your schedule. There are natural benefits to boosting posts or creating content as adverts. Facebook has the most advanced platform for targeting specific audiences. Exploring and going into the real depths of how to harness this marketing tool fully is a whole other book in itself. However, due to this being a constantly evolving platform the written content may soon become out of date.

If you wish to learn about how to harness this fully to grow your business through specifically targeted adverts, my advice would be to seek out a current Shopify Store Owner. There's a whole community of Shopify owners who use this as there main scaleable marketing tool to sell new products and they have very in-depth knowledge which they need to ensure is current in order to compete, failing that, there is great content constantly being uploaded to YouTube.

However, simply boosting your posts it's fair to say you have very similar powers although operating on a lot smaller scale. Boosting / or FB Ads offers a powerful targeting tool where you can narrow your audience through segregating: gender, age, location etc...dive a little deeper and you can go into the depths of whether they have recently started a new job, specific interests, in a new relationship or what kind (dating, married, divorced etc...). It's scarily powerful.

So taking into consideration this kind of reach and specific targeting ability we can look over our draft posts and messages we have created and think whether any of these would really benefit from boosting. We have to bear in mind it's easy to soon start spending money doing this so it's good to ensure our posts meet the right criteria in order to gain the best possible return from investment, or simply start testing the water with smaller budgets and then being quickly scaling up on posts which gain a strong initial level of engagement. This could always be a mentality to use on currently published posts, ones with strong levels of recent interaction could be prime candidates for boosted content.

Note:
Personally I have experienced lower Reach on organic Facebook Page posts when I have gone through a period of heavily Boosting a series of posts. One would assume this could be a trait within Facebook's algorithm to have made me feel more inclined after seeing those results to spend more money and get back in the cycle of heavily boosting posts. Makes good business sense, however, please note this is my speculation, however, have seen this a multiple of times. I have found best practise to be select a couple of key posts to boost and not everything to avoid this.

Best practise when choosing posts to boost is choosing ones which have a good life span. (for example not for an offer which expires the same day as posting). Choose something which is engaging and has the potential to lure people to comment, tag friends in comments or generally attract likes. There are two ways in which we can gain real value from boosted posts.

One is the traditional driving traffic to a specific action where you can convert into a sale, whether it be driving them to a page where they can book a table in a restaurant or through to your commerce store where they can purchase your products.

The other is by growing your brand presence and audience. This is through driving brand and post engagement which is why we suggest choosing a post which is worded to drive an action of engagement to help push the post to go viral. This is where we start treating the paid Boost literally for what it is, a boost. We use it to help kick start the initial engagement and from there it can be left to organically grow and flourish into the beautiful flower of a post attracting bees to it to interact.

These two ways give us a measurable to which we can compare our ad spend and justify by breaking down our cost per engagement or cost per click / conversation. It gives us valuable data to asses and learn from our campaigns so we can adapt and evolve them which is something we shall go into properly later in the book.

Reflecting back to our spider diagrams with our post messages listed. It's good practice to circle the ones in which we are considering boosting so that these stand out to us.

Just when considering the post run through the checklist based on the above:

- Lifespan
- Traffic or Engagement
- Is it worded to encourage the desired reaction?

Marrying our prospective Content with our schedule

So we have our spider diagram with our themes and post messages, we also have our draft schedule with boxes of when and where we plan on posting. Suppose the done thing would be to marry these together and formulate our plan.

Let's start by looking at our themes to see if any are date relevant. Maybe you're pushing a series of content relating to an event, an offer which ends mid-month or maybe it's February and you're doing something special for valentines day. These type of themes would take priority and it would be good to map these out onto our schedule first.

Themes which would take the least priority would be Brand or USP related posts. These are more like fillers, despite caring an important message however they are not pushing a direct call to action or urgency.

So starting with our Sales Event in our example case,

let's say this Sales Event ends on the 20th. This means naturally it's pointless posting any of these posts after that date. Next to look at is whether any of the individual posts / messages are specific date critical. For example, a post stating: 'Ends Tomorrow' is fairly self-explanatory in regards to where it should sit within our schedule. Work through the rest of the posts within this Theme to see whether there may be a chronological order into which they should be posted to whether match any other date critical criteria or to whether there is a story been played out throughout the post content. For example, if it turns out we are playing out the story of the Three Little Pigs in a twisted new campaign for a bacon burger it would be daft to send the Big Bad Wolf to the House made of Brick first.

When plotting our posts on to our schedules as well as looking for specific dates we need to understand our posting content to see whether it's something we wish to condense into a short space of time say a few days to tell a more immediate story or to see whether we spread our themes out across the month. Where possible it's good to mix and match our posts to offer our audience a variety of content as not everything maybe something in which they engage with and keeps your feeds seeming fresh.

Sometimes alliteration can be effective. Maybe you have two posts on the same Theme you wish to use on the same day to enforce the message and drive that conversion, using one to reinforce the other. With these though it's good to write them like a good British sitcom. The story follows on however you're not left lost if you missed the previous post/episode. The first example here which springs to mind is planting the seed for order a takeaway.

In the afternoon you can post your teaser offer to spur the interest and plant the seed and entice the craving. This can be lunchtime, hit them while they're hungry however can't order, you hit them when they have that feeling of hunger, trigger the emotive message. You could then follow up the campaign and hit them when they finish work and chances are again hungry. Here you could play the devil on the shoulder. Use a really enticing photo of your food, fire in the background and the wording 'Give in, you know you want to, pre-order here...'

It's succulently evil.

Work your way through your themes and place them on your schedule. A good way of doing this is to number the posts of your spider diagram. Means it's quick to swap around and make changes. Assign each Theme with a highlighter colour and simply put a dab against each box near the timestamp. This offers a quick representation to the spread of our themes across our schedule. We can see if we have a balance of content being spread and bunched together to create a certain desired impact.

This is always something which you will find yourself tweaking as you go through, as you'll come across one message and realise it would work fantastically in a time slot you have already filled. It is worth remembering though that the times we set earlier aren't set in stone. This is where you can tweak these to better fit your content and help deliver your message more effectively.

Section Three

Create

Creating Content for our Schedule

We have formulated our planned out schedule with our various messages, in here we have a break down of all the content in which we require collating or creating to finalise our posts ready for publishing.

We can run through these schedules and formulate a list and categorise the required content. Some useful categories to break your content requirements down into our:

- Links to Articles
- Photos (Onsite)
- Photos (Offisite)
- Video Content
- Article Pieces

From here we can tackle these as manageable tasks.

Gathering links to external article sources or linked

content can be a good starting point as can be a quick win to tick off.

In the following couple of chapters, we shall look more into the approach for capturing and producing the desired photo and video content for our posts.

By taking a structured and planned approach we can minimise the time spent and develop this process to be a natural part of the business in which we can even involve and begin delegating to teams members. This opens the doors for more creative input and minds to collaborate to help create more enriched content.

We may even nurture our own and our team's mindset to become very proactive in regards to content creation and seek opportunities for Social Media Content during daily tasks and capitalise on this and capture the content when it presents itself.

It's a great habit to get in to and taking short video snippets of business operations or scenes which showcase your business in a good light can become very useful to keep on file and have on hand. It saves the time and expense of having to go back and try to recreate these natural moments when they're required to help enrich one of our messages.

Tools / Do we Outsource?

They're naturally two options here and the key is not too be scared and jump straight to outsource. Don't get me wrong there are always occasions where outsourcing is definitely the wise choice however it is surprising how much in regards to content creation you can produce in house.

I always find it more effective producing content in-house purely because it goes back to the routes of nobody knows your products and services as well as you do. However, admittedly there can sometimes be occasions where insight from a consultant or third party can help you extract the key points and help showcase them in a different light.

Thankfully we live in an age wherein our pockets lives a very powerful device which will outshine a full-blown production studio of the past. Of course, I'm talking about our phones. Whether your team Android or team iOS, either way, you'll have the power to take high-quality photos and videos to showcase your business. I have previously taken a majority of business social media content on my iPhone purely for the ease of use. The ability to be able to post directly from my phone or air-drop to my Mac for editing is just far easier than fumbling for a cable however that's personal preference. One big benefit of using a modern phone over a basic point and shoot camera is the image processing power for digitally enhancing lighting etc...With low lighting shots, the phone will win.

Note:
Some of the newer phones with multiple cameras are worth having a play with. These are very effective at focusing on certain objects and in some cases have the ability to alter the focal point of the image when editing after. Great for blurred background shots.

The benefit here is you don't need to feel like you need to go out and spend a load of money on a high-end SLR Camera in order to get the ball rolling. Now don't get me wrong these do have their place and do show a natural improvement in quality. If you were creating photos which may be used in high-quality print publications or if you are very proficient in photography and understand how to make the most of these cameras and there features then fantastic. Naturally, these have a bigger lens and sensor in which to capture light.

In regards to my personal setup, I have a pair of SLR's. One is dated now however has a long zoom lens which is useful, was great back in the day doing motorsport photography. Another which I use for HD video and product photography when I set up a studio, portable tent and lighting etc...I have another mid-range point and shoot camera which lives on a gorilla pod and I used this for planned video content. It's rugged, easy to chuck about, I'm not too precious if I write it off and have been known to wrap it around a lamppost and risk leaving it whilst I get a drive-by shot. Other than that 85% of any content I use for social media whether that be photo or video comes from my iPhone. I personally find its the perfect balance between quality and quick accessibility for shooting content.

In essence, the message here is that for the most part we already have the tools we need for the job and we are already empowered, we just need to be creative and embrace them.

Now admittedly I'm always one to be guilty of buying kit because I feel it would empower me to create something when in the most part I always harbour back to the simple kit mentioned above. I have also purchased a 3 axis gamble camera before and for the most part, these are fun to play with. When doing smooth panning shots or walking with the camera, these are incredible for ironing out any stability issues and if it's something in which you are going to make use of on a regular basis then is something I would recommend. Just aim modern and midrange is my personal advice. Issues I had with an older device was connectivity and battery life.

If you are going down the route of video and speech audio is something you wish to use on your content then I would recommend something with an external microphone. Makes for a lot crisper audio feed. Again this is where high-end smartphones over shadow point and shoot cameras for internal audio capture as a lot of them have multiple microphones in an array for audio clarity on phone calls, an aspect already heavily invested in for its primary purpose.

The other stand out piece of kit which enables you to capture an aspect which other kit isn't able to do is a Drone. Mid-range professional drones these days are fantastic production tools and the imagery offers a whole new depth to your content. Again these are great to use as a toy however it's worth considering whether you will be able to regularly make use of this tool and use it to create valuable content in order to justify the investment. Expect to spend £400 plus on a quality entry-level drone. Below that you're still looking at toys.

Now back to the original point in question, do we outsource. Yes, you do have the majority of the tools already in your pocket to create fantastic content. For small to medium-sized businesses especially if it's still content you are producing for social media content then it makes more sense to keep the focus in house. May even be a bit of fun if you have a professional photographer come in for the day to work with your team to teach you and them some skills to improve your mobile photography skills. A good team building activity and one in which you can use to elevate the quality of your content.

However, in respects of larger businesses targeting a more national or global audience, chances are you'll have sufficient budgets at your disposal for marketing content and it is then worth having a professional take on the task. This is where you will also probably have large marketing teams and some of the approaches of this book may not be entirely relevant. However, this level of professional content may be out of reach of budgets for regular content however maybe a consideration for special projects for key promotions. You may wish to compete with John Lewis in the battle of the Christmas Adverts, this is where the quality video production can stand out. It's also easy to assume high-quality video production is vastly expensive and in fairness, it can be. But certain smaller projects you may even find a student or a budding hobbyist is able to create you something wonderful and a professional standard on a relatively low budget.

I will throw out there that one small to medium-sized business sector where from experience I have found it greatly beneficial having a professional videographer rather than undertaking in-house is in the Bar and Nightclub industry. Purely because of the editing ability and working in challenging lighting situations. The skills here really come into there own and I personally find this the mark of a good videographer if they can shoot a good nightclub video.

Capturing and producing quality video content is naturally a lot more challenging vs capturing photo content for your business. Short single clips can be very easy to knock out yourself however when it comes to more complicated editing this is where developing your skills or seeking some help could be useful. It can be a fun creative project to play with creating a video for your business if you have the time to do so. For a small business having this skill set on tap can be very beneficial if you were in a situation where you needed to produce quality video content at short notice or on the fly. Is a topic where there is lots of great content on YouTube.

Plan sessions for Content creation

A little bit of planning here goes a really long way. This is the stage where if we aren't proactive in our approach it's very easy to start wasting time running around preparing shots on the fly and it's easy to have even paid models sat around simply costing you money, and nobody wants that.

The best way to avoid wasting time here is to sit down with a completed content schedule and break down the requirements for each piece of content and see if we can group the creation. In the most part, we shall be creating photo content to accompany our posts and a fair portion may be conducted on site.

The key things to pick out are:

Location, are these taken on or off-site.
Photos on site generally speaking can be condensed into a single shooting session. Photos off-site do take a little more planning and shall look at this in more detail

shortly.

Do any of these photos require models to pose in them?

This can be broken down further to whether or not we can use the same model(s) in these shots, naturally it would make sense to group the photos using the same model, in the same location together.

Do these require any products which need preparing?

Do we need to arrange for specific out of general prep hours for team members to be made available to help facilitate this shot or is it something which could be conducted during normal business hours, a restaurant environment is what naturally springs to mind here and do we require a chef to come in early to prepare a dish for a photo.

You may even find you can outsource some of your content creating to your team. Again I shall use the restaurant example here. If you were to leave a brief of what you are looking for in your marketing content and especially if they've seen examples of what you expect this can be a great way to integrate them into the process of showcasing your business. In this respect, it also gives them another talking point with customers.

They can suggest a product and add the backstory of really craving it during the photo shoot yesterday, it was like torture. Adds that extra bit of depth to help them up-sell a desert maybe. However, from a practical point of view chances are you may require a chef to be on shift to produce dishes which can be used for these photos. Let's say for example the downtime between lunch and dinner service would be a great time slot in which you can accommodate this. You will also have team members available on shift who can be used to act as models. They'll have quality cameras on their phones or you can either leave them a camera so you don't need to be there and this becomes almost an automated part of your business so you can concentrate on other things. It's also a great excuse for team building and giving them a sideline project to help them feel more valued. You could even get to the stage in this scenario where its that scheduled it's on your weekly jobs list and you simply give them a checklist.

One thing I have found effective before is by using methods like this including the team it empowers them and during downtime, they'll take the opportunity to practise their photography skills and can help you build up a catalogue of images or even post content on their own platforms to help showcase your business. An example springs to mind of a member of a team I previously worked with showing off their Latte

Art through Instagram and tagging the restaurant.

In some aspects of your content schedule where you have Off-Site photo requirements, you may find you need to incorporate your team into this. Let's say you're a building or installations company and your products are showcased off-site. In this scenario, it would make sense to use your team while they're there to save on additional travel costs. Simply train them on how you like to see certain products showcased and then give them a list of the portfolio shots to take after they complete a job. This can alter the approach from specifically scheduling time / trips for your content creation and begin turning it into a natural part of business as a normal activity. This helps you consistently and constantly build on your marketing content.

You could even plan your posting schedule around forecast completion of certain key jobs or projects. For example, you may be installing office furniture at a well-known client in the middle of your forthcoming posting schedule and you can leave a placeholder ready for this enabling you to showcase this relatively swiftly after sign off. This helps keep your content current and relevant. You simply arrange for the team to send the photos over soon as completed, or even send over some work in progress shots (just make sure no health safety breaches in these, shows you in a bad light). You can get these photos approved by the client to post and you're ready to go and have them live before your team makes it back to base.

Some of your required photos could be from remote locations where your team don't plan on visiting. You may be a bag company and want to get photos of your products in locations all over the world showcasing them in a travel scenario. Friends and Family going on holiday could be a great opportunity to produce this type of content, simply lend them some bags for the week. Other options may include connecting with people through Instagram who travels a lot either as a brand influencer or as a photographer for example. Supply them bags and some pocket money in exchange for a few casual photos of your bags in action as they travel around. If your bag is designed for a specific use it may be worth picking on people within this niche and approaching them to really showcase the USP's of your product. It's all about reducing your costs for creating content and making it a more natural and sustainable business activity which offers immense benefit and minimal impact on your time.

Of course, you may have very deep pockets and feel it would be far more fun to travel around the world yourself and photograph your bags coming off airport carousels. To be fair if my lottery numbers came in I know which I would choose for the hell of it.

Failing the above options for capturing remote content this trick would be to map out a cost-effective route or method to tackle these tasks. Its just worth taking into strong consideration the potential return on investment here and justify your actions and spend on producing this content. It's for a business at the end of the day and if you can't justify a business case for this kind of marketing content a rethink is needed.

Let's pane back to the use of models. You may have chosen brand influencers from social media who fit your brand to showcase for products for Off-Site Content however when creating On-Site content it's very easy to become sloppy and just use any Tom, Dick or Harry. We always need to ensure our models reflect our desired target audience. This allows our audience to connect with them and in their heads exchange themselves for that situation and creates that emotive connection we spoke of before.

More often than not we will have team members who reflect our targeted demographics and they're happy to get involved posing for a few photos. Other options are reaching out for professional models, however here we need to consider budget and need to ensure all of our shots with them are condensed and planned effectively to control time and costs.

There may even be someone who works in a local business who would work as a great model for your photos and opens the opportunity to find an angle to collaborate or cross promote in some shape or form. You may have noticed I'm a fan of finding ways for local businesses to work together.

But Could you cheat?

In regards to capturing and producing content for social media, there is always a Plan B. That's cheating. You could go down the orthodox route of using Stock Image sites, just ensure you understand the licensing limitations of the content you are purchasing. There may be a limit in types of usage of that image, just worth bearing in mind.

The thing here is to ensure the photos pictate your business, product or service in the right light. Admittedly for Service-based industries this can be an easier and more effective method of gathering content. Lots of photos of Suits around a table out there. What you need to consider though is the long term portrayal of your business. Is there an infinite number of these on brand photos realistically using the same core models for consistency purposes. Makes the story seem more believable, just be prepared for a client to ask to meet the girl in the photo (If she's in every boardroom meeting photo), an easy excuse is 'Unfortunately she left the business' or just be honest and say they're stock images.

However, there are some great tools out there which can really make this art of faking brand content very easy. Admittedly I have used these for a start-up business previously when launching a fashion brand. I was planning on using Instagram as a large focus of my marketing campaign and required a vast amount of content. Organically this would require me ordering huge amounts of T-Shirts of various styles and sizes, arranging photo shoots, going to locations and capturing the content. For a start-up project, I was trying to kickstart on a limited budget this was soon a method to become a money pit and sink the ship before it set sail.

I came across a company which would create mock-ups of models wearing various T-Shirt designs, with a nearly bottomless catalogue of photos to use all for a monthly fee less than me purchasing 3 T-Shirts from my supplier to use. It became a no brainer to get the ball rolling. This allowed me to have a workflow where I could create a design and have marketing content for it Live within 10 minutes of completion. That's something hard to rival in the real world. Admittedly these sort of packages I'm sure become very scary if you're a wannabe model.

This doesn't only work for T-Shirts, out there are various different sites who offer this style of service for a variety of products. This also opens the potential of creating a series of photos of your product and giving them to a designer on Fiverr to Photoshop these into real-world scenarios and create your content that way. The possibilities are endless.

Of course, if given the opportunity to create effective real content for your business social media platforms this should always be the route to take. However, this is always an option worth considering the costs due to being insured for creating such content start escalating somewhat. Getting a photo of your bag at the North Pole to promote some new artic design becomes a very costly exercise unless to cheat slightly.

Edits / Post Production

Photos

In regards to photos in many circumstances our raw content is enough, although maybe a cheeky cropping with a few minor lighting adjustments and colour tweaks here and there to really make them pop. We have the choice of whether the photo itself speaks enough words or do we need to overlay a few more for it to be able to really shout out your message.

Cropping

This is where you can trim an image to kill two birds with one stone. If you have a high enough resolution image along with being able to trim items from photos you'd rather hide or are not relevant. It opens the possibilities to crop a Contextual shot down to a Hero Shot and then even down to a Close Up shot. This gives you a breadth of options if for any reason you're having second thoughts regarding your initial intended shot.

Lighting / Colour

This is where Instagram is a great one to play and experiment with. You could opt down the route of creating a unique branded style of images and distinctively edit them or could just play with more subtle tweaks to enhance them slightly to make them eye-catching and vibrant. A personal tweak I tend to lean towards is increasing the Brightness and Contrast by about 20%, Find this works well with a majority of the photo content I have worked with recently. It's worth trying to be consistent in your editing so you create a recognisable brand feel for your content, more so with the more distinct changes you make.

Overlays

With overlays its always worth considering the posting platform. With Facebook, these can work well, Twitter it's worth considering our image sizing for best view (currently it loves shrinking down, however, the interaction to see more could play to your advantage, worth thinking about) and then in regards to Instagram, I would say personally no overlays for posts unless its a theme in which you have amongst your previous posts. However Instagram stories, Yes. It's a good place to shout things in my opinion.

Our Instagram feeds are a precious one. It's a post editing world of style and consistency, most of which editing and modifications we can undertake through the app itself. There's no right or wrong answer here, its about finding a style which works well and reflects your brand values. Only thing I will suggest is to try and maintain consistency with your editing approach with this platform, it's very much tailored towards being a pretty place.

Some people regard overlays in general as a big no no however in certain circumstances they prove very effective. They, of course, need to be designed in the right way, a consistent theme in which represents your brand is best to practise here. An example of use could be a photo of the front of your shop and an informative post regarding changing your businesses opening hours. It could be a good idea to overlay these new times on the image so they jump out as users scroll through their feeds.

These photo edits and overlays can be easy to administer yourself. Some may opt for Photoshop as a default editing program however for the simple changes and additions we are looking to add it can often be overkill. Simple vector based or basic image manipulations programs would be more than sufficient. You may find editing apps available for mobile devices to be the best tools for the job.

Video

With video post-production soon becomes a lot more complex due to the variety of elements and pieces or raw content in which come together to produce the end result.

If your a novice there is a selection of available tools and apps which can help you put together short pieces of marketing content for social media. Simply search along the lines of 'Make a video for Facebook' and you will get a list of these and is worth exploring what each has to offer to get a feel for the type of content you can produce.

You could opt to use iMovie, for example, create a short video. One trick I find which works well for short showcase or story videos is stripping the audio from the video and replace with a backing track of relevant vibe. This helps cut out any background rustling or conversation picked up when filming.

If you are more proficient in video editing then further tricks, software and methods for editing you'll be well aquatinted with and this isn't the book to develop those skills.
However, if you are looking to edit your content or produce into something more substantial than a single clip or two while still maintaining a sleek professional feel this is where outsourcing could become an option. A student with good video editing skills could be a good option or if seeking something very high level and your budget permits, a professional videographer is the direction to head.

They'll have a whole host of kit and great concept ideas for shots and how to piece them together. Even just watching their process, seeing some of their raw shots and then seeing the end edited result can be a great learning curve and give you ideas of how to tackle smaller content projects of your own in the future. I've found this when 3rd parties have been into create collaborative content where I've had to be in front of the camera, watching how they piece the building blocks together in the edit can be rather enlightening, especially when you notice they've seamlessly spliced together multiple takes.

Section Four

Publish

Do we use Automated Tools? Pros & Cons

You'll be familiar with a variety of the automated posting tools outs there, many popular ones have names which you would decipher were originally designed for use with Twitter. These all have similar abilities where you can queue up a series of posts ready to release to the world and it will work its way through posting them at either specifically given times or to meet your pre-defined posting schedule.

Sounds like a dream. Doesn't it? Well, I personally have had mixed experiences and specifically prior to writing this book I embarked on trying a fair few of them out. This was because there a lot of new kids on the block in this space and I wanted to see how they'd evolved. My main focus was something I could adapt this methodology to and the main focus on being having a clear to use scheduling platform at the heart of the system.

In all honesty, only one I like and not even got a side deal in place to mention it, however, it's 'Planable'.

Slightly pricy however worth it based on its ease of use and transparency alone.

Though let's look at these tools in general and key features to pick up on. With many of the traditional tools, it was always a case of you would compose your message, attached a photo and tick the boxes for which social media platform you wished it to be published on. As from what we have learnt in earlier sections of this book there's a glaring problem here with this. Different platforms showcase our content in different ways so we need to tailor and format our content accordingly. So being lazy and clicking post to all is a massive pet hate of mine, almost as bad as single sided flyers and business cards (if dropped wrong side up its just another scrap of paper). Once this is something you are aware of you will spot these type of posts a mile off and it's tragic to see unfortunately and is so easily avoided.

This biggest piece of advice I could offer and it is to take the extra few minutes by composing and scheduling posts for different platforms separately. It will make the world of difference in the long run and how people perceive your business.

It's worth experimenting to see how well your choose

platform handles video scheduling to Facebook. This is something in which I have seen mixed results of success and during some instances, I found this something which was easier to achieve by going direct with facebook and scheduling the content from there. Having the ability to properly complete the Title and Tags fields for video content helps this medium of content become more accessibly discovered.

Another thing worth experimenting with is a strange one however I have found over the past few years through various accounts and tools makes a noticeable impact. This is to take note of the post reach on Facebook for scheduled content using your chosen 3rd party tool compared to posting directly through the platform. I have seen many examples in the past where I was receiving unto 80% lower Reach through 3rd Party scheduling tools. If this is something you discover this could be a possible root cause. Is a strange one however for example if the 3rd Party app is using a slightly poorly configured API Facebook may deviously choose to steer you away and back directly into their eco-system? (Now this last part is speculation however would make sense).

When playing with some of these scheduling platforms you may have noticed one social media platform appears to lack comprehensive integration support?

Instagram. As a platform, it makes it very challenging to automate content publishing. You can understand why, it would be far too easy to spam post to a certain hashtag to get your brand seen. Plus it would eliminate you being able to make use of their editing tools to polish your photos finish for dare I say 'That Instagram Look. It allows for a platform to consist of more organic and natural content of hopefully more relevance.

You'll be pleased to know there are some tools out there, like the one I mentioned earlier which do allow a certain level of integration with Instagram. However, as opposed to automatically posting for you it offers more of an alarm clock style feature. An accompanying app will Push Notify you, download the photo and copy of the Post text to your clipboard then allow you to easily paste it into your post. This sort of thing is a great stepping stone however if you're managing multiple accounts your forever going to be stressing over posting scheduled content and if you're like me with multiple Instagram accounts signed in simultaneously you just need to take note where you're posting. Risky when half awake posting at the crack of dawn, and ones a Sex Toy Website.

So I have droned on about some negative aspects and things to look out for, however, it has to be said, if you are planning on posting consistent regular content to all your social media platforms and also see the light of day one of these tools is a must. It's just down to you to choose which is right for you. Yes, they all vary on features, allowances and costs, though at heart provide a similar function.

You may even find you come across a tool which allows you to eliminate the glorious Pen and Paper from our previous steps and give you the ability to plan and map out your post content going forward live on the tool. This would eliminate the risk of losing or spilling coffee on stray pieces of paper and with some also allows the ability to delegate access to different projects and platforms allowing you to offload some of the workloads to your team and give them the opportunity to become more involved in the marketing process, especially if you are a small team. Those that operate in this manner generally give you the option to approve, comment or reject proposed content allowing full transparent control over what messages and content in which your business in publishing to the world.

From a business owner and management point of view, something like this soon becomes invaluable and going back to the initially raised question of should you use such a tool, Yes! The key with social media is quality and consistency and with the best will in the world maintain manual consistency will honestly run you into the ground, and that's what this book is trying to avoid.

Interim Content and Changes

Now it's all well and good planning all of our content a month or so in advance, it makes for a good night sleep. However what if something important happens or just changes, does it just go unnoticed and then put off to the following month. Thankfully not.

Can you imagine if the News companies did this when planning their content to post, our breaking news stories wouldn't flag up until a month later, would play havoc with weather warnings. These types of media companies will have a pool of general feel-good stories or national stories in which they can tap into on a slow News day, or around here simply show the Police chasing Swans and then not understand when the whole town trolls them with Hot Fuzz quotes. Then they are able to post stories on demand to a degree as and when it happens, with a fall back prepared.

The best mentality is to treat our social media scheduling plan more as a framework. This provides us with a consistent feed of regular content in which we can post. We have to understand and appreciate that life is complicated and things do change so we have to be able to adapt. Let's say something big happened and took priority over your planned content. It's a Wednesday and you have two scheduled posts primed and ready to go out:

12:00 - Post 1

18:37 - Post 2

It's currently 17:30 and you are about to publish your Live post. Naturally dependant on what your other posts are in relation to dropping an extra post into that schedule isn't really going to hurt things. However, does open a couple of option here for you to consider. Do you simply remove 'Post 2' and in essence simply replace it with your current content and 'Post 2' either drops off the schedule all together or pushed forward to the following day. Or do you asses whether it would greatly affect 'Post 2' to be pushed back an hour to allow you to spread your content a bit better allowing these posts each a sufficient timeframe and opportunity to reach prospective users without treading on each other's toes?

A couple of options always worth assessing when this situation arises, however, a decision only you can make at the time purely because this will be greatly affected in what's going on, what the specific content in these posts is and how altering their broadcast will affect your business and the information portrayed to your audience.

This also showcases another clear benefit of using an automated tool to centrally publish your content as it enables these last minutes changes and tweaks to be addressed swiftly. May even be a case of click and drag the group of posts down the timeline a fraction to accommodate and saves you frantically logging in and out of various profiles to asses and make potential amendments

When publishing content on the fly another thing which is worth taking note of is the rest of the scheduled posts you have in your queue. By placing this off the cuff piece of important content does it cause any impact on upcoming posts in regards to contradicting them or making them irrelevant. You may have just announced a Festival has been cancelled due to unforeseen circumstances and then scheduled for tomorrow is a post promoting ticket sales.

Your schedule is always something worth reviewing on a regular basis just to ensure a small change within your business hasn't affected any upcoming content. You may have an upcoming post scheduled with an insight into one of your valued employees however you could have sacked her the week before for secretly turning off the staff room fridge at night to make everyone ill. (I know right, what a bitch). This soon becomes an invalid piece of content and is something worth being prepared to address before the content is automatically set free into the world.

Basically, it's just worth considering the bigger picture when the need arises to publish unscheduled content and ensure they're no greater impacts and almost proof check what's going out.

Links and Short Links

Posting links in our posts are something we should only do if they prove relevant and it is the intention of the post to drive traffic away from social media platforms to this other content. For example, if you are showcasing a product, the link could be to a location in which a user can purchase the item, leading them along your sales funnel.

However, links to most products listed on e-commerce sites tend to be rather long-winded and clutter up our posts making them look messy. We're looking for clean and sleek. All the gibberish within our link contributing to a length worthy of a high score on snake simply takes away from the prime Content real estate where we could be convincing people to click on the darn thing or be allowing us to embrace the philosophy of 'Less is More'. (Think Twitter, they count the characters)

There's a couple of ways in which we could approach this. If using Facebook we could have the option to embed the link out of view within a 'Shop Now' button (I say could as the platform is constantly evolving). Or the other more common approach with we could use on other platforms such as Twitter could be to shorten our links.

Now, this isn't a case of deleting a bit for fun and hoping for the best. You've no doubt come across these mystical links. Often starting with: bitly..... This is a common website where you simply copy and paste your horrible cumbersome link and magic happens and you are presented with a pretty short link in which we can use within our posts.

Of course sadly magic doesn't really take place here, basically they place the link in their database and spit out a condensed link in which we can use and they'll then route our traffic for us in the right direction. By allowing them to route the traffic also poses another benefit. They can count the times they have to provide this action.

We can now easily keep track of the number of times in which users click on our links in our posts allowing us a method to measure their effectiveness. Because of this, it's always worthwhile creating an account on such sites to enable them to store and keep track of this information so we can reference back to it later on.

What if we were to go one step smarter and allow these sites to create links for us individually for each different social media platform where we are posting the same content? This then allows us to keep track of where our traffic is coming from and measure which types or styles of content perform better on various platforms.

Now I understand each social media platform has its own built-in tools for tracking this type of information however this simply gives us a second reference point so we can compare to ensure accurate results and offers us the ability to easily compare the results between platforms in a single location for a quick glance.

Tidy links and extra analytical benefit…is essence it's a win-win! Simply search 'short links' in Google and a handful of sites offering the service will flag up.

Note:
A post without links scores better in the social media algorithms. This is because it is not leading you outside of their eco-system and in essence you are still a customer to display advertising content to, which is where they make their money.

Try not to Publish and Forget

It's fantastic being able to publish a month's worth of social media content in one go. However, it's good practice to not simply click publish and forget. Printing a copy of your publishing schedule and making available to members of your team and for your own reference is invaluable.

You may have published an offer which triggers a real-world interaction. From a business perspective you don't give out a very professional image when you publish something and a customer walks into your shop having no knowledge of what the customer is talking about. It's key to ensure social and real world combine and communicate with each other.

I've had it before from a restaurant perspective where I have just left site and seen someone whom I know's in there tag a photo on Instagram. I'll take a screenshot and text over to a member of staff working (preferably one I know has a bad habit of subtly checking their phone). This empowers them to be able to make comment with the customer and is able to thank them, saying just seen and really like it for example. Builds that connection in the real world and offers a talking point.

It also allows staff the ability to be proactive and prepare. For example, if you're a bar who has scheduled a promotion of Gin and Tonics for the following day going live they can stock check the number of limes on site, act accordingly and ensure have allocated enough prep time to slice a few extra ready for service.

There are limitless examples of how making the published social media schedule available benefits. It also offers that extra opportunity for team input. They may spot a glaringly obvious opportunity which for some daft reason you have overlooked. Offers the chance to address and capitalise on. Communication and Teamwork, make the dream work!

Section Five

Analyse

Why Analyse?

Why take the time to analyse our results? Surely it's more time effective to be creating content rather than spending time looking at numbers and graphs? This could be true, however not if you're out there creating the wrong content for your audience to connect with your business.

We create a given piece of content for a reason. At heart, the reason is to promote our business and grow them. We then broke down areas of our business to promote through creating and choosing certain Themes in which to focus on. These had a goal and our messages were then a string of outlets in order to help us engage and drive traffic to achieve these.

If we're not looking back to see whether we have won or not, why are we playing the game or creating this content in the first place? Chances are we haven't been able to put out the very best content we could, we've put out some good content however chances are with our ever-evolving audiences and competition there is some room for improvement. This is where looking back and analysing our results comes into play. It allows us to ensure we are creating effective and relevant content.

The various social media platforms all have a range of tools and metrics in which we can break down and evaluate to assess our results. This is where we can begin to introduce real-world statistics and financial data to offer a real comparison and realise our return on our investments for creating this marketing content.

This is data which we can suck back into our business as a core and establish how well our products or services are being perceived. We may be able to run very similar campaigns for two different products and see that one is selling and the other simply isn't. This could outline an issue with our product as opposed to our campaign and content. This allows the opportunity to tackle this matter more directly and establish where the core issue lies. It demonstrates a business case to drop a particular product or adapt it to suit.

Through looking into this data we can seek opportunities and market places to push our business further. We may find a gap in our audience demographic which our product would perfectly suit.

For example, you may find you have a very small audience in certain large cities compared to others, this could trigger the opportunity to run a targeted paid promotion in picking on these locations to plug this audience gap. Assessing your demographic you may find a high level of engagement however spot a potential to increase your conversion rate. You may wish to support this social media campaign with a billboard for example within this specific area to help nudge up conversion, going back to the 7 points of marketing to convert.

As you can see there is a whole host of benefits in relation to spending the time to analyse these results. I understand it may be a chore which you may feel more inclined to embark in if you were hosting boosted content because you can physically see a cost associated with each post. It's always very easy to overlook the investment and cost incurred in producing the content originally. This is a cost worth evaluating to discover our return on investment as well as ensuring we are developing as much return and value as possible from our posted content.

What can we look at?

All of the 'Big 3' platforms have in-depth analytics to allow us to measure the successfulness of our posted content and track our campaigns. With them all, we can track how many people interact and even physically see our content. These are stats in the most part we can track relatively in real time and allows us to grab a quick progress snapshot of how our posts are performing.

Facebook

On Facebook, the key things in which we can monitor during a given period are:

- Page - Likes, and growth of these
- Total Post Reach (Paid / Organic)
- Total Post engagements
- Total Video views (over 3 seconds)
- Basic Audience Demographics
- Call Action on Page (The button we set at the top,

usually to 'Send Message')
• If Pixel installed - Track Orders and Earnings from traffic

These items where we can see the totals across posts naturally we can dive into these more specifically against the individual posts and see clear breakdowns of these engagements:

- Likes
- Post Clicks
- Comments
- Link Clicks

Post clicks is sometimes a strange one to interpret however it basically summaries all click interactions with your post, whether it is clicking on the photo to view or expand the comments to read more for example. It's a good indicator for how eye-catching your content has been because sometimes people are strange and may like your content however not wish to put their hand up and say so, in other words, tap the like button, give you an indication at least.

Twitter

With Twitter we can capture a month by month breakdown however when logging into our analytics we are created with a rolling 28-day snapshot offering us data on:

- Number of posted Tweets
- Total Tweet impressions
- Profile Visits
- Number of mentions
- Number of Followers

Other stats available include:

- Our Top Tweet (impressions)
- Our Top Mention (one with most views/interaction)

Of course, all of these stats again can be broken down to a tweet by tweet basis so that we can evaluate individual performance. One key feature currently is when assessing our audience. Along with the current location demographics we are able to see the popular interests of our followers. This can be useful when planning content and trying to plot an angle to incorporate these themes into our content to spark interaction. If 97% of theme like dogs, could you have a personified dog as the character in your post. With the Bag company example we used earlier, we could have a photo of the dog modelling the backpack. This would have a high potential for tapping into this audience.

Note:
To enable Twitter analytics on your tweets you will need to visits the analytics site to enable. Simple Google: 'Twitter Analytics' and look for the twitter domain and login. You can then on the app see the impression against each individual tweet you post.

Instagram

With Instagram using the app we can gather a 7-day snapshot of our pages activity. This includes:

- Total Number of Interactions (broken down by day)
- Total number of Profile Visits
- Total Number of Website Clicks
- Total Number of Contact Button Clicks
- Our total profile Reach (Unique Accountsl)
- Our Total Post Impressions

- Follower Growth

Note:
If you wish to track over a longer period it would be worth seeking a 3rd party Instagram Analytic tool to harvest this data and keep track.

We can also then dive into our individually posted content and story content and view the Reach, Impression and breakdown for where these impressions came from. We can also see further interaction for example if using Instagram Shopping we can track product click-throughs and see how many users whom were then enlightened to view our profiles to learn more based on that particular piece of content.

As with other platforms we are of course able to gather a location, age and gender demographic data of our audience. We are also able to see when our audience is most active so we can plan our post timings accordingly.

One thing which can prove very insightful if you're one to pay very close watch of your stats, is when posting Instagram stories we can see exactly who has viewed these. This can be useful to spot trends of regular viewers of your content and track to see whether this follower converts into a sale, however, this is something you'd have to track more manually and currently not a tool within Instagram to monitor this directly.

These platforms as you can see all offer great insights into how our audience interacts with us and when analysed in the correct way can prove to be a powerful tool to help us refine our marketing content to attempt to squeeze further interaction from them.

Did our Posts Perform?

This is the heart of what we are seeking here. It's also worth noting early on that if we do come across one of our posts which haven't hit their targets and haven't performed especially well compared to our others this can be a vital insight to investigate and be very useful for ensuring future positive results.

The best thing here is to look back at our Themes and think back to what we were originally trying to achieve with these messages which we posted.

Of course on the surface, an easy situation to mark as a success would be a festival in which we were selling tickets for and the tickets for the festival Sold Out. This may be something which seems like a waste of time analysing the data for. However, we can look at which platform drove the most traffic towards our ticket links, break down the demographics of audiences and look for potential growth opportunities for hosting a follow-up event and the most effective way to promote the tickets for it.

Our goals on a basic level for our Themes commonly would be to:

- Drive Traffic (then convert)
- Attract Engagement

As well as these basic theme related goals we may have global goals for example:

- Increase sales / conversions by 'x' % or hit 'x' target
- Increase our following/page likes by 'x' number to develop our audience.

We could look at the audience question more in-depth and look at growth in certain locations or in other demographics.

Drive Traffic

Our posts with the intention of driving traffic can be easy goals to asses. Simply take note of the number of click-throughs from that post, is there many or is there few? The thing to determine though is what you would consider a good click-through rate. This is the percentage of those our post reached that clicked our post link. This will vary greatly between products and industry. I like to say anything over 1% is good starting block to aim for. If a post is not achieving this it's worth comparing reactions and click-throughs on other posts. If other posts are strong, this highlights a poor piece of content. If you are seeing low results across the board then it's worth analysing your audience.

If we have a series of posts within a theme each driving traffic to the same location it's worth ranking them in order as a list and then trying to identify key differences between those which performed highly compared to those which performed poorly. Factors to consider could include:

- Type of image (hero, close up)
- If a close up was there a key feature which gripped your audience?
- Format of wording
- Manor of wording (formal, informal)
- Time of day or even the day in which you posted

These are all factors which would impact how the post is perceived,

The key is to pick out the best features which contributed to good performance and aim to focus on these merits for future posts to help increase conversion.

Engagement

Judging post engagement could be a bit more subjective.

There are a variety of ways in which users can interact with our posts. Naturally the more interactions the greater the reach generally achieved by our content. This is because the social algorithms will deem it as a piece of content of interest and will push it out to related users to discover.

This again is where we need to look back at our original message to determine whether there was a specific goal here. Was it a case like an earlier example I gave which stated ' Tag your boss'? This was in relation to "Big Burger' and trying to encourage your boss too to buy the team lunch. This here was driving comment reaction to aid in reaching a larger audience and jovially promoting the use of emotional blackmail by employees to their boss to trigger a large sale, thus promoting exposure of the food products in this scenario to a large real-world audience. Is an example with very much exponential reach potential through social media and real-world audiences.

In this example, the metric to measure would be comments and then analyse these through visually scanning through the comments and seeing the tags and sparked conversation within. With this example again you would have to determine what you would classify as an acceptable result. It may also be worth considering real-world results and looking at sales figures or communicating with the team to see whether any of these nature of orders took place within the week or two following this post going live. This would be how you go the step further to track the conversion here.

If you are seeing positive results from your social media campaigns then fantastic. Whether that be you are seeing an increase in footfall and physical sales in your locations or traffic and conversation online the key now is to look at opportunities in which to capitalise on the success and scale these results. If you have found key pieces of content which are proving very effective it's worth on your following social media schedule almost replicating the post and content and introducing a paid boost to help increase its reach. If its a post driving engagement you should hopefully see your organic growth begin to grow exponentially as these paid viewers are organically tagging others in your content.

Of course when it comes to analysing either of the above goals against your results you need to ensure you have a fair sample of data in which asses from. If your posts are only reaching 150 people then you simply don't have sufficient data in which to draw any logical or meaningful conclusions from. This is where you need to be reaching audiences of at least a couple of thousand to be able to pull out any significant insight into post-performance. Of course, the larger your post reach the fairer assessment and more accurate the statistical data in regards to looking at percentage based figures.

If you are only achieving low reach figures, it would be worth investigating ways you can boost your pages following, paid promotions, collaborations or competitions probing engagement can be great starting points.

So whether or not all of our posts have performed or not we can at least take away some action points from here to develop our businesses further.

```
All Naff ——— Reasoning? ——— Audience Size ——— Paid Boosts, Collabs, Competitions
                              Audience Demographic
                              Product ——— Engage with target audience for product feedback.

Some Good ——— Identify Best & Worst elements on messages and content ——— Formulate new super posts to drive big results

All Good ——— Indentifly best performing to scale to larger audience ——— Capitalise on Success
```

Did our Posts Perform?

Analysing our Audiences

Are our social media audience reflective of our target audiences?

This is a key question to be reflecting upon. If you're an online business with global shipping the world is very much your oyster however you will still naturally have a few key location demographics in which you design and target your content posted towards. If you're a local business you naturally what to be able to hone in on a specific town or region.

If you are seeing a poor conversion rate across a few of your posts this is the first place to begin analysing to ensure your audiences match. You may find you have a strong audience in Asia, now if you are targeting a UK or US market, for example, this could pinpoint you have a large number of fake followers. The kind of dormant ghost followers promoted through social media bots or through the purchase of followers through some dodgy shiny website for a handful of dollars. (Great for kick-starting the impression of your page, worthless to you after that).

If you're pitching to the wrong crowd they're not going to bite. For example, people in cold countries buy fluffy hats, not inflatable Swans to lounge around the pool on.

From our social media analytics we can harvest the basics:

- Location
- Gender
- Age

These are great for establishing core demographics. For example when looking at gender and we're selling bras. Generally speaking, not many men purchase bras. So if we are looking at a high percentage of male audience chances are they just like to look at the photos rather than purchase your products.

These metrics, however, don't give us an insight into the interests of our audience. (Unless you're looking at twitter). This is something you have to judge through reactions to your posts. In regards to organic followers, it's safe to say there is at least some interest in your business, product or industry. However, if we look at the Big Burger example from earlier, being able to determine the percentage of our audience being Vegan is something we will have to take an assumption off based on our niche content interactions to posts relating to our Theme showcasing the 'Unbeeflevable' burger. As a whole we can say organically they would be based locally to the restaurant, have an interest in food and like burgers however, the specifics we have to dig a little deeper and interpret.

At core going back to the question at hand it would be worth looking at the metrics we can pull from our social media data and outline for each of these our target audiences and establish where a majority of our real audience is sitting and compare how closely these align.

We could discover from here that we have strong performing posts and our business is making good sales however these audiences are not aligning. Here it's worth having a look at available sales data and it could be that we misconstrued our original target audiences and in fact, our product appeals to a different demographic. This is where some market research with your original target audience is worth looking into to asses your market positioning and to consider when developing future content for your social media platforms.

We could see a split. We could see 50% alignment to our target audience and 50% highlighting an unexpected demographic. This new demographic could be something worth trailing targeted content with to test engagement. This is something where you could create two identical boosts on a post where these demographic variances are the variables we change. This would allow a controlled way to measure and test this audience compared to our originally outlined target demographic to see whether it's worth tailoring our content to attract this group when developing further post content.

Changes / Improvements

There is always the opportunity for constant improvement in regards to our social media content. Our competition and audience are always evolving and keeping us on our toes trying to judge the most effective approach. Keeps the game entertaining.

The trick is to stay on top of the curve and have the vision of what's to come. Tracking how our content performs compared to our competitors is worth taking note. We may have spotted some of their posts has taken social media by storm and is getting significantly greater engagement that one of yours. Well whats the saying, if you can't beat them join them? Let's comprise on this and take some elements of this strong content of theirs and see how we can harness it in some of our own, and then beat them.

Understanding what is performing well from ourselves and our competition and outlining the merits of poor perming content is what allows us to adapt and survive. Sounds primitive but in essence, it's true.

You may find different combinations of these elements work better than others. You may choose to create the ultimate social media post to test the system.

Taken the most engaging posting time slot, theme and content type and package all together. In theory, this should then provide strong results. If this works then try to focus on these elements throughout a majority of your posts. I wouldn't say take these and embed all of them into every one of your posts because this rules out the opportunity for experimenting and testing new content and discovering changes in engagement across the platforms. It may be a case you find certain content traits become more effective on certain platforms. This allows you to begin differentiating your content more in which you post to the various platforms to maximise results based on how that specific platform delivers.

Don't be scared of change, trying something new and mixing things up a little from time to time. Just keep track of what you are changing and track average variances within post-performance base upon these. This empowers you to continue refining your content in this positive progressive manner.

Seek the ingredients which work well, learning to use

these as a staple in our recipes going forward and drop and changing these as performance fluctuates in order to asses whether these key elements are still proving their relevance.

Think like a football team, swap out the players as and when to ensure you have the best goalkeeper, defence and attack possible for the team you're up against.

Through this method of change and improvement we should be able to keep our content engaging for our audience and provide the ability to convert.

Side Topics

- A brief look at SEO
- Scaling Campaigns
- Hashtags
- Being Successful on Instagram

A brief look at SEO

SEO in detail is a complex and ever-evolving practice because as the types of content available, how we consume it and competition out there evolves, staying current is a constantly cycling which is adapting however there are some core fundamentals which I can't see changing anytime soon.

It's far from the good old days of the early naughties where would simply put a few keywords in our page header and have a fighting chance of being ranked. Competition is a lot stronger and the bar has been raised. There are numerous factors which come into play here. In another topic, I speak about the Instagram algorithm and that's a walk in the park compared to the ranking system Google have in the background to help us search the world's content.

At the core, a search engine is about offering the user quality, valuable and recommended content on a given subject. This means that a quick overview of key weighting factors can include:

- Page Titles

- Page Description

- Page Content

Note:
Keyword relevance and density within the 3 items. Whether keywords or phrases are falling within various page headings again offers various weighting to their relevance.

- Whether your content is updated regularly to keep it current (where a blog comes in)

- Whether you have social media accounts linked within your website

- How popular are you within these various social media platforms, this provides a social ranking of your business or brand.

- Is the content on your website social media friendly. For example, are you making use of metadata and tags to pick out key content to make it easily sharable within social media platforms? These each have their own formats of how they portray the content of a link and if you haven't defined for various platforms what can be used as the Main Image, a Title and a Short description then this will affect your ranking. It's thinking of how well your content will be portrayed to show relevant information and display when shared on these platforms.

Note:
When sharing article or blog content on your social media platforms it's worth checking the links display properly. If they don't chances are these meta tags are not configured correctly and it looks like you are sharing a poor piece of content, Sadly on Social Media people judge a book by its cover.

- Backlinks. This is an age-old concept and is still as relevant as ever. Are quality reputable websites linking back and referencing your website. The old days simply linking your website within a series of directories to build the number of your backlinks was sufficient however now Google has the power to properly asses and rank each of these. Being referenced in well-known blogs and viral content on social media is a great weighting factor here as shows strong support for your content. Again more reason to ensure microdata for social media is enable to help your content on these platforms.

- Load Speed, Nobody wants to be waiting ages for their content to be loaded, if your too slow, Google won't want to be recommending you, simple as that.

Note:
In regards to loads speed, it doesn't offer merit to fast loading pages, it simply discredits those who are particularly slow.

Search Engines have also involved to pretty much understand the words we are using and can create associations between types of relevant content. So instead of just looking at the specific keyword it can analyse and suggest results based on relevance to the core subject matter or build content value based on the weighting and relevance of other immediately linked content. There's no real easy games and trick we can throw into the mix to trick these intelligent algorithms.

The secret is to be organic and product relevant and informative content regarding your subject matter. Again this is where blogs can really help boost the value of your website, it's creating a library of relevant and valuable content to deem credibility towards your website.

If you make sure your website takes into account the

above criteria you're on a good starter for ten for being ranked well within the search results. For further details on how to improve your websites ranking further check out YouTube, lots of great current detailed content.

Scaling Campaigns

This is something we touched on briefly during the Analyse Section of the book and was looking a scaling in regards to finding a successful piece of content and finding ways to capitalise on its success.

Normally when people talk about scaling campaigns they're normally originating with a paid boost and aren't just growing something which was achieved results organically.

If you were to dabble with paid content alongside your regular organic posting schedule it's always best to start small and test the waters to see what works.

Using the Facebook Ad Manager you can create a series of tailed adverts with bespoke content targeting a variety of different audiences for your industry or product. This could be used as a tool to gain business insight to help establish your core demographic to focus on pitching your product.

Let's say for an example we use location as our variable and create 5 posts targeting 5 different locations.

Note:
When playing with post targeting from a paid perspective as we mentioned earlier we can go very in-depth so it's always worth playing with the demographics to see the size of your potential audience.

We are going to choose:

- Manchester
- Leeds
- Birmingham
- Northampton
- London

We place a £5 advertising budget against each and we allow the ads to run for a period of 3 days. Upon analysing the results we find that Northampton and Leeds as locations to target as they performed highly. The others not so much. For this campaign, we are seeing that for whatever reason these are receptive areas so the logical thing would be to increase our budget slightly for these two and see if we receive the same percentage interaction and conversation realists as before.

If as we increase our budget we maintain the same strong percentage interactions or it's even increasing the logical thing to do would be to scale up the campaigns for these areas until you exhaust them. Just ensure you keep note of the figures and remember to downscale when these begin to drop else you could see yourself quickly squander your profits in wasted advertisements.

Take note of the product and results for future reference and then begin testing other demographic variances and take this same scaling approach with each testing sample to asses results.

It's the safer way of trying to promote your products without spending vast sums of money on areas or demographics which may not be very receptive and cause you to simply waste your marketing budget. The more niche and refined you're targeting the better this approach can work and the higher your conversion rates for successful campaigns.

Hashtags

With original origins dating back to the 70s with use in programming languages, the hashtag was very much reinvented back in 2007 through the use of Twitter as a way to categorise content.

Seen almost geeky in their infancy now hashtags are openly used as second nature as part of daily life for many of us, however, used more for the use of gaining social gratification rather than intentionally categorising our content.

Hashtags have evolved into a key part of social media marketing on platforms such as Twitter and Instagram. They used to attract viewers of similar content through searches and from those following specific tags, inadvertently categorising our content.

Instagram especially hashtags have become a spamming parfait to lure users towards our photos in the pursuit of likes. Instagram allows a limit of 30 hashtags to be included in a caption (however you can always cheat and squeeze a few extra with the first comment).

This gives a lot of room to define your content and is now something in which demands extensive research to use effectively and deem whether or not your chosen hashtag is relevant or a regarded as a 'cool' search item. A common one for fashion bloggers is #ootd which on the surface seems like gibberish however stands for 'Outfit of the day'. Some are evolving from simple keywords to in essence forming keyword phrases like '#motivationmonday'.

You want to look for a hashtag which is:

Relevant to your photo and find a balance between those which are swamped with associated images and those with a limited number. This means you have the potential to hit the volume hashtags attracting millions of users where competition is strong and have the balance of lower completion hashtags where it's easier for your photo to stand out. This balance means you are covering a variety of different angles to allow your photo to gain traction and develop its reach.

Taking the time to research and look at the types of content and how often content is being published within these various hashtags gives you a good assessment of how you can use them and leverage them to your advantage.

When trying to think of relevant Hashtags to research it can sometimes be challenging. Thankfully if you hop on Google and search 'Hashtag Tool' you will be greeted with useful tools which can search the current relevant hashtags within your niche or industry. Some results will seem fairly common and like no brainers however, some of the results can appear a little obscure (worth a search first before using).

Most of these tools are free and advert funded however some more in-depth hashtag research tools may indeed want to charge you a monthly fee. Worth seeing how you get on with the free tools and scale up to that approach.

You will see those who are very successful on Instagram rarely use Hashtags, like famouses for example. Purely because they have such vast audiences they don't need their content to be discovered in this manner to aid it in gaining traction. It's mainly your middle tier of users who seek to capitalise on the advantage of using properly researched hashtags to broaden their discovery.

Using effectively can be an essential part of growing your audience on these platforms.

Being Successful on Instagram

Instagram is a platform worth taking an extra look at. It has quickly evolved to become one of the most popular social media platforms out there with a high level of user engagement.

To grow on Instagram it's about ensuring you understand how the platform works, publish good quality content and that how present your profile with a keyword mentality in mind.

Ensuring you have a clean descriptive bio is the most effective way to convert profile visits into followers. For example below is a current copy of my personal account.

As you can see I have made use of Emojis to act as a visual description of the content and kept to key effective elements. I then make use of a pointing emoji to divert attention towards my website. If you tell someone to do something they're generally more inclined to do it. (As a man should never admit this but nagging secretly works)

Algorithm

It's very easy to assume the Instagram algorithm to be a scary daunting thing to try and understand. It's the word algorithm which is off-putting. It's too easily associated with complex mathematical problems and they can just make your head hurt.

In essences, it can be mapped out as a very straight forward acceptance process of how to displays and ranks your images.

At its very core it works like this:

- We post a photo of a tree for example.
- Instagram then shows these images to your loyalist followers to judge their reaction, you know, to test

the water. It defines your loyalist followers as those whom Like or interact with a majority of your content. If it gets the seal of approval from these users it then pushes through to the next stage.
• Here Instagram will allow your middle tier followers to view your photo. The ones who interact with some of your content. Again if gains acceptance from this group it proceeds.
• The algorithm will then push your content through to those who follow you and rarely or don't interact with your content to see if it can get a reaction from this group. If a portion of these users begin interacting the algorithm then decides this must be a really good photo of a tree and thinks maybe this content has the potential to be accepted by a wider audience.
• Here is where Instagram starts a similar process by pushing your content out to the Explorer Pages through select groups of users at a time, ones who like very similar content or user accounts to your self. You know, safer bets firsts before exponentially pushing your content out to more and more users.

The reason for it being geared in the gentle structured approach is for example if it just pushed everyone's content out instantaneously the quality of the content seen on average would be really poor. Let's be honest, some people do post some real tosh on Instagram. By using this method your Photo has to gain acceptance from a variety of different tiers each, in essence, a tougher crowd than the last in order to be released freely. This is why sometimes photos in the Explorer pages are a day or two old because they've had to go through this process. Other newer content would be naturally deemed a safer bet to push through because the user has had a string of successful content working through these various ranking stages before and its deemed a safe bet for auto-acceptance.

Of course, this is only the core process. There are of course a whole world of other ranking factors which begin to come into play. It then operates very much like SEO Page Ranking and they consider backlinks. This means the individual user accounts who are interacting with your content also offer various different weighting to the ranking score of your post. A user account interacting with 100k followers is going to offer a more valued judgement of your content in regards of the algorithm as opposed to a new account with 27 followers, no profile photo and likes and follows everything in sight.

It's a rather straight forward process once broken down and the trick here is how can I cheat the system and nudge my way towards the Explorer pages faster. Of course, there is a way.

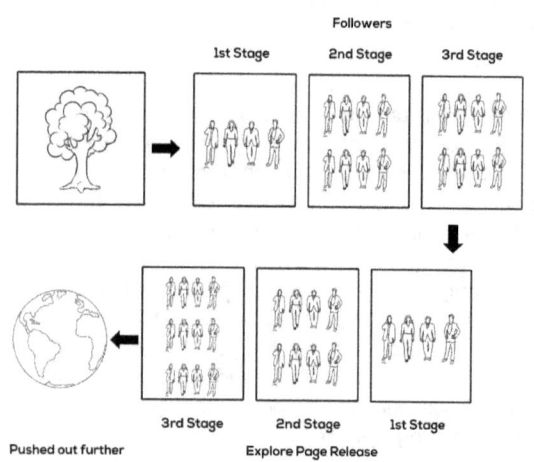

Power Likes

Power Likes is how we intercept the Instagram Algorithm and dare I say slightly cheat the system and give your content a little boost in the right direction. So the interception points are the mid-tier of followers who interact with some of our content.

The way of doing this is setting up DM groups and networking with other users with accounts in a similar niche to your own. Again those in a similar niche offer that extra weighting to the ranking factor, its kinda taking the assumption these accounts must know what they're talking about in regards to rating / liking your content. Simply start messaging other accounts and build a rapport and invite them to your DM Group. In these groups, you can have unto 15 users. Key is to aim to have a multiple of these DM groups active and target users if possible with more followers than yourself. These are basically treated as 'like for like' groups and you can notify these users of when your plan on posting they're content so they can get in early with the likes giving your post that initial buzz and traction.

This, when done properly, can be good for gathering a hundred or so likes however we want to grow exponentially and hit the Explorer Pages.

The next step is to hit random users and I can't give you an exact placing for how these groups of user interactions will sit within our algorithm flow diagram, however I would assume they would be staged towards that 3rd stage of followers and rarely interacting users.

There is a messaging app called Telegram and on here hides a whole host of Instagram power like groups. These groups can be found through searching google for 'Telegram Instagram power like groups' you'll get links to invite yourself to the various groups from there.

These groups are administered by bots who strictly monitor your interactions and remove so-called Leaches from them, normally 5 strikes and you're out. There are groups for various niches, a minimum number of followers and various levels of interaction. Each has their own rules so worth reading these to learn how they operate before diving straight in. Some of these groups have upwards to 20,000 active members so offers a good pool of users to boost your interactions to that next level.

Now there is always no guarantee that after doing this you will make the Explorer pages however it's a step in the right direction. The easiest way to see whether you have been successful is to keep an eye on your Post Insights and it will be listed as a separate Reach category and the rate of your post interactions will generally begin to increase significantly.

Using Bots to Grow

This is where in essence you are treating the notifications section on a potential followers phone as an advertising window where you want to get your brand name. An easy way to do this is to interact with this user in some shape or form.

However, targeting these users and issuing these interactions on mass can be vastly time-consuming and will very much sap your life away. This is where bots come into play and if you search Google you will find a host of these. (I like Combin)

Basically, you can target who you wish to interact with through searching Hashtags or seek those who follow a specific user (or competitor). These will then conduct Like and Follow interactions for example with your define audience while aiming to stay under the radar of Instagrams anti-spamming policies. These are tools which are quickly evolving so more relevant content will be found online (or on my blog, I reference these a lot).

By defining a clean and informative profile, publishing quality content, cheekily manipulating the algorithm through Power Likes, using bots to reach out to your audience and then organically interacting with other users in your niche you are following the recipe to organically grow and develop your audience on Instagram.

Instagram is a platform which has intrigued me and I have recently spent a lot of time playing with to understand it's mechanics. Here I have only touched the surface on how to grow on the platform because its ever-evolving, however, these merits are something to follow to help achieve success in building your account. I've had an account with basically no content published, a fake brand, clean bio and occasional use of a bot grow to 800 engaged followers in a short space of time. This is little effort and proves results are very possible.

Final Thoughts

I'm hoping that through the journey of reading this book you've felt inspired to come up with a few creative ideas of content you can use to promote your business. Discovered new ways to showcase key unique features of your product and brand to engage your audience.

You feel confident to take that step back to avoid being a bull in a china shop and ensure you take a structured approach to create a social media plan and creating your content.

Find you are able to produce a consistent stream of effective content where you can begin to see growth within your results and don't feel it be an endless chore and it is becoming a more natural and organic process within your business.

We have only focused on using this for the 'Big 3' however nothing stops this being applied to other platforms or marketing outlets. So why not give it a go!

Space for your Notes
(My publisher makes me put some blank pages in so knock yourself out)

www.ingramcontent.com/pod-product-compliance
Lightning Source LLC
Chambersburg PA
CBHW060833220526
45466CB00003B/1082